W. H. Auden at Work

W. H. Auden at Work

The Craft of Revision

Alexis Levitin with Joshua Kulseth

LEXINGTON BOOKS
Lanham • Boulder • New York • London

Published by Lexington Books
An imprint of The Rowman & Littlefield Publishing Group, Inc.
4501 Forbes Boulevard, Suite 200, Lanham, Maryland 20706
www.rowman.com

86-90 Paul Street, London EC2A 4NE

British Library Cataloguing in Publication Information Available

Library of Congress Cataloging-in-Publication Data Available

ISBN 978-1-66692-294-3 (cloth)
ISBN 978-1-66692-295-0 (electronic)

Alexis Levitin
For My Mother, Isabella

Contents

Acknowledgments

Alexis Levitin

I would like to thank W. H. Auden, my mother, Isabella Levitin, and Joshua Kulseth, without whom this book would not exist.

Author's Preface

Alexis Levitin

BRIEF COMMENTS ON THIS UNEXPECTED BOOK

I was a young ABD, teaching at Dartmouth. Three years of Greek Tragedy, Shakespeare, Milton, Conrad, Joyce, E. M. Forster. Even Dostoevsky. Pure bliss. The best years of my life. Then, still an ABD, I taught a full year of upper-level Shakespeare at Tufts. Another year of happiness. But my chairman pointed out the obvious: "You cannot go on without a PhD." Four years of blessed good fortune coming to an end.

I was in love with James Agee, but my savvy mother foresaw an endless biographical/critical pursuit that could easily lead me into a role we all know from Chekhov: the eternal student. She strongly suggested I seek a narrow focus, something I might efficiently bring to a swift conclusion. I could think of nothing.

A close family friend, even wiser than my mother, came to dinner. "Wystan," she said, "Alexis needs a clearly defined, circumscribed topic for his doctoral dissertation so he doesn't drift on forever. Do you have any suggestions?" Wystan had great respect for my mother and sent her all his poems before they ever appeared in print. At the time of this dinner, he had just published some co-translations he had done with her of poetry by an unknown Czech poet, Ondra Lysohorsky. The poems appeared on the first pages of *Poetry* (August–September 1970) but alas, my mother, Isabella, was transmogrified into Isobella Levatin.

"Yes, I do," he replied. "How about a study of my revisions of my Sonnets from China?" I squirmed a bit, since I had never read the source of those poems, *Journey to a War*, the collaboration that sprang from Auden's trip with Christopher Isherwood to China during the Japanese invasion just before the

1

onslaught of World War Two. I sat there silent, but nodded an embarrassed assent. And that was that.

Perhaps I ought to examine the motives of the three of us. My mother's motive was clear: she simply wanted to help push me toward a doable dissertation, so she could finally say, "This is my son, the doctor!" (my mother was nothing like that, but I can't resist a terrible Jewish joke I know would have made Wystan laugh). My motives were even clearer: How could I even think of disobeying my mother or turning down W. H. Auden, a man whose breadth and depth of understanding so overwhelmed me that I considered him a creature from another realm. As for Wystan himself, his motives were mixed. He was irritated that critics had attacked him for his revisions, claiming he was trying to revise his past, rewrite history, pretend he had never been a communist sympathizer in his youth, etc. He hoped my dissertation would reveal his revisionary practice as that of a master craftsman honing his poetic skills, deftly manipulating words, compressing language, sharpening images, replacing the general with the specific, the fish with the trout. And indeed, that is what my study focused on: the craft of revision. I was not an apologist for possible changes in content, changes in world view. I simply ignored those larger questions of meaning, of intent.

In any case, when summer came, I gathered up my Olivetti portable typewriter, the original *Journey to a War, The Collected Shorter Poems, 1927–1957*, in which the final revised versions of all those sonnets could be found, took along twenty books to read for pleasure, and drove to Maine. I returned to the remote lake where I had spent all my childhood summers. With a sleeping bag, a bathing suit, some shorts and a sweater, a towel, a flashlight, some matches and cans of peanut butter and tuna fish and a couple of loaves of bread, I hopped in a friend's sturdy old rowboat and slowly made my way to Gooseberry. It was a tiny island of moss-covered rocks, pines, hemlocks, spruce, and a soft undercoat of pine needles on pleasantly spongy loam. Its shoreline was bursting with blueberries. It was inhabited by several chipmunks and squirrels, its surrounding waters patrolled by emblematic loons with their deep and penetrating cry. I would live in the simple cabin with no electricity but with a sturdy little writing desk. I would work all day and would swim around the island to relax. I would drink water from the untouched lake and eat my humble sandwiches till the book was done. It was a vacation of dedicated labor that would nourish both body and soul.

I worked my way through the sonnets methodically, much as my mother and Wystan had envisioned. I did about five pages a day, noting every single revision I could find, grouping them into categories, trying to understand their purpose. I would swim around the island, then return to work. I would read *Native Son* for a few hours, then get back to work. I would munch on a peanut butter sandwich, then get back to work. Once in a while a young neighbor from across the lake came roaring out in his motorboat, bringing cards and a case of sodas. We would play gin rummy, drink a soda or two, laugh a bit, then he would roar away, and I would return to work. At night I would crawl into my sleeping bag, light an oil lamp and read for a while, then go to sleep listening to the haunting cry of the loons. In the morning, I would brush my teeth in the lake, then get back to work. During those four months I learned most of what I know about the craft of poetry. The nitty-gritty of how it works and what can make it work better. And after those four months, as crisp autumn days began to arrive, I saw to my surprise, and perhaps even regret, that I was done.

I submitted the dissertation in the fall, it was duly read, I was awarded a distinction and now possessed the obligatory PhD. However, I suddenly noticed I had no money in the bank. I had paid a typist $500 to type up the final version of my study, and I had paid Columbia University $500 for the right to make my defense. No money and no job, just a freshly minted PhD. And cold winter was coming on. So I said to the secretary of the Graduate English Dept. "Do you know of any job offers? I'll go anywhere in the world."

"No, she said, "there's nothing." Then she pulled open a drawer and called me back. "Yes, here's something that just came in." It was a fax that said: "On an island of lush green rolling hills, with thirty-seven spectacular white sand beaches, the Federal University of Santa Catarina in Florianopolis, Santa Catarina, Brazil, is looking for a recent Ph.D. in American literature to help us establish a new graduate program in English and American language and literature." I knew nothing of Brazil, but I needed a job and liked beaches, so I applied. Three weeks later there came a simple telegram: "Congratulations. Stop. You have been chosen. Stop."

And thus the rest of my life was determined. The road not taken would have been to hunker down in a cheap apartment on the Upper West Side and convert my dissertation into a book. That is what any sensible graduate student with a new PhD would have done. But I looked at the telegram and wrote back. "I accept. When should I arrive?" I never gave my dissertation another thought, and two months later I was in Florianopolis, starting a new life.

I lived in Brazil for nearly three years. My house consisted of an airy complex of rooms facing a broad lagoon filled with shrimp. I had a carpenter build me a small rowboat, blue and white, and it bobbed gaily at the end of my dock. My neighbor was a shrimp fisherman, like almost everyone else in the village and, like everyone else, he was illiterate. He had wonderful carriage for an old man and casting his net he looked like a modern dancer reaping the universe. It was in this idyllic spot in the austral spring of 1973 that I received my mother's letter telling of Wystan's sudden death. It was a shock. The man who knew everything, who understood everything, was gone. I was not a poet, but upon hearing of his death, I wrote the following poem, which later appeared in *The Anglican Theological Review*. It is the only poem I have published in my life.

      For W. H. Auden

      The shaggy bear
      his corrugated face
      a contour map
      of all that glades
      and forest can contain
      is gone.
      The sun weakens.
      Forgotten forest thickens ranks.
      A chill breeze trifles with us . . .
      Then the air stands still.
      Uneasy, glancing at the shadows gathering round
      our little glade of green,
      we understand, now, what it means,
      to live upon a slowly cooling planet.
      The shaggy bear
      our guardian beast
      is gone.

After less than three years, my graduate program successfully established, I returned to America, having found Brazil too heedless and hedonistic for my Puritanical leanings. Back home, I began to translate so as not to lose the lovely new language I had learned. Half a century passed, I published close to fifty volumes in translation, mostly poetry, and never gave my old dissertation a thought. It was, after all, the road not taken.

And then I received a phone call.

"Hello? Is this Alexis Levitin? Yes. Good, my name is Joshua Kulseth, and I am in love with W. H. Auden's poetry. I love everything about his poetic voice, his precision, his formality, his efficiency. While pursuing W. H. Auden, I came across your dissertation in the archives at Columbia. I think it's terrific. You really should publish it."

I was astonished. "Joshua," I said. "I am flattered that you like my work. But I wrote it fifty years ago and have never thought about it once since then. I am now a retired old English professor. My career, such as it was, is over. Wouldn't it be absurd to publish my first scholarly work at the age of 80? A joke, don't you think?"

He didn't think it was a joke and, thanks to him, to his drive, his insistence, and his faith, here is the book in your hands. The dissertation comes to you exactly as I wrote it half a century ago, not improved or embellished by the dubious wisdom of my accumulated years. I will rest content with Auden's own response to my youthful essay (see figure i.1).

I learned a great deal about the craft of poetry in writing this study. I hope the reader will also come away from Auden's masterly practice and my analysis with a deepened respect for *poiesis*, the making involved in the craft of poetry, that soughing musical branch of linguistic art.

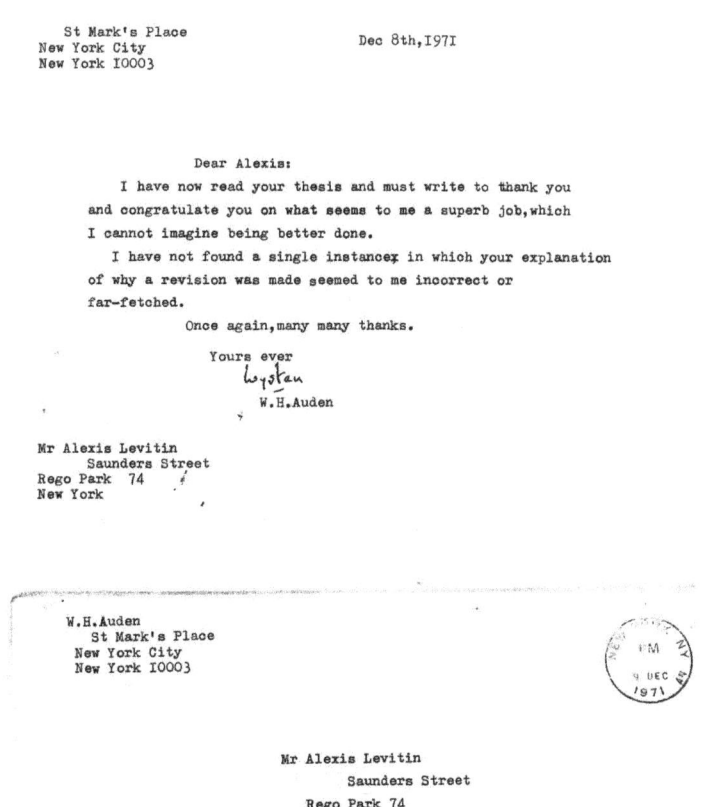

Figure i.1.   Letter from W. H. Auden to Alexis Levitin, December 8, 1971. Provided by Alexis Levitin.

Reader's Preface

Joshua Kulseth

I.

My initial contact with the poetry of W. H. Auden came by way of his much-anthologized poem, "Musée des Beaux Arts," where the banality of the rural scene is juxtaposed with the fabulous plummeting child Icarus. This first meeting was unremarkable, my only recollection of the classroom scene the still vivid memory of the peculiarly worded (and unpoetic sounding to my tragically opinionated 18-year-old mind) "doggy life" of dogs. I can still hear my teacher's voice, the way she seemed to mirror the cadence of what I imagine now must have been Auden's intended nonchalance. I should note I found it unremarkable not because the poem is, or that my wonderful instructor's lesson was somehow defective, but rather because poetry in general was still entirely outside my purview. At the time I was far more interested in the seriousness of philosophy and theology than of what I perceived to be the silly, navel-gazing, mulling-over of language in poems. And if I was interested in poetry at all, it was in its occasional functional moralizing (the kind one might find in Dante, Milton, or Pope). All the rest was baffling, and as I see it in the hindsight of my now-profession, frightening. Much like Breughel's sailors on their "expensive delicate ship" passing unhelpfully by the floundering white legs of the drowned Icarus, I had "somewhere to get to, and sailed calmly on" (Auden, *Collected Shorter Poems* 123).

Auden snuck up on me the way a friend might, when after years of touch-and-go association, one day you find yourselves to be inexplicably inseparable pals. Even after poetry became for me what I can only unironically call a vocation (I smile now writing this, knowing Auden would likely smirk approvingly), the purse-lipped, prune-cheeked Englishman wasn't the one I might have guessed would become my most well-loved and consistent artistic companion. I was too attracted to the alliterative melodies of Hopkins and wild imaginative mythologies of Yeats to notice it was actually the quiet, tender insistence of Auden's verse which was enlivening and defining my experience of poetry.

He was laced, scattershot, through my undergraduate education, most notably in an introduction to creative writing class, where his other famously anthologized poems, "In Memory of W. B. Yeats," "September 1, 1939," and "As I Walked Out One Evening," saturated my imagination, along with others more obscure, like his gently ominous villanelle "If I Could Tell You," or the painfully incisive ballad meter narrative, "Miss Gee." I couldn't quite put my finger on what kind of poet, or even what kind of man, this W. H. Auden was, and agreed for a little while in this bemusement with a professor who had dubbed him a "poet's poet," meaning, somewhat derogatorily, that he appealed only to a limited subset of ivory-tower, poet-academics. You know the type: the ones who prize obscurity and technical proficiency above, let's say, the more approachable, colloquial verse of a Larkin or Heaney. It's absurd to me now that I ever believed this about him, and it's an opinion which certainly didn't survive long into my devouring of his *Selected Poems* during the summer after my junior year of undergraduate studies.

I wish I could recreate for you, dear Reader, the uncountable hours of befuddled delight I spent poring over his slim collection of *Selected Poems*, and later, the much more robust *Collected*. I wish I could, even for myself, revisit those moments of original joy at newly discovered gems of verse, which were for me at that time like a balm for what I had incorrectly perceived, though no less felt, was the trite cynicism of post-modern and contemporary poetry. I fumbled to make meaning out of the near-mythological landscape of his early poems, peopled with familiar characters (a soldier, a banker, a spy) but expressed in a fantastical lexicon and perhaps deliberately entangled syntax. I would learn, embarrassingly enough to admit now, only much later of Auden's encoded world and the secrets to deciphering his early work. But for the moment it was enough for me to soak my bones in the delicate strength of his language, the assuredness of his convictions no less tender for being steadfast. And of course, it was Auden's ability to turn a phrase, especially at the end of a poem, which kept me pleasantly occupied:

> Noises at dawn will bring
> Freedom for some, but not this peace
> No bird can contradict: passing but here, sufficient now
> For something fulfilled this hour, loved or endured. (20)

*

Yours the choice to whom the gods awarded
The language of learning, the language of love,
Crooked to move as a money-bug, as a cancer,
Or straight as a dove. (80)

*

O stand, stand at the window
As the tears scald and start;
You shall love your crooked neighbour
With your crooked heart. (85)

*

. . . Some may be heroes
Not all of us are unhappy. (100)

*

Lay your sleeping head, my love,
Human on my faithless arm. (107)

*

To fresh defeats he still must move,
To further griefs and greater,
And the defeat of grief. (118)

Much like Auden's own secret world of hidden meaning, encoded and set before the reader without apology, his verse engendered in my imagination a world of words, and as Eliot insisted of any good poem, I felt what they desired to communicate long before I began, finally, to understand them.

Though I respect the material dignity of books and cringe when I spot a dog-eared page disfiguring the paper of a used copy I've picked up somewhere, I will admit to frequently abusing my now almost entirely decrepit copy of Auden's *Collected Poems*. In fact, and this is something I imagine he might find amusing, its physical state now mirrors the portrait which graces the cover—that of an old, disheveled poet whose skin resembles more the texture of a steamed potato than of a human.

It was my constant companion for many years, and in the rough-and-tumble bowels of my school backpack it rested beneath notebooks filled with the entirely mediocre poetry I'd tried my hand at, most of which imitated one form or another I'd lifted from Auden. It is marked through with notes: questions mostly, but frequent comments, and even the occasional and unnecessary exclamation "Hah!" leveled at one of his witticisms or particularly funny lines (an example immediately springing to mind comes from a stanza in his "Letter to Lord Byron" where he successfully rhymes "poet" with "know it"). Curiously though, and I wonder about this even now, when I turn to the section of the book devoted to his "Sonnets from China," my scribblings trail off, leaving many of the pages almost entirely blank, with only the occasional exclamatory "Wow" to punctuate my original amazement.

Surely Auden wrote better poems—though this particular sequence, composed during a youthful quasi-journalistic trip to China with his friend and collaborator Christopher Isherwood in the midst of the Sino-Japanese War of 1938, is still even by Auden's standards technically and narratively awe-inspiring—and it's unfortunately true that none of the sonnets made it into the popular anthologies where his other works are found (likely one reason is that to be taken at all, they must be taken as a whole). But nevertheless, in my own mind at least, where his arguably greater poems hadn't prevented the graffiti of notes I spread along the margins, his "Sonnets from China" had done just that.

I write this introduction not with the sole intention of expounding learnedly on the exact value of the sequence for a broader readership, or for its equal value as a learning tool in classroom discussions of poetic revision—both of those will be addressed, briefly by myself, and much more extensively by the author of this volume, Alexis Levitin. Rather, I'm writing for you, dear Reader, a record of my *wonder* at these poems, in the hopes that you too might wonder with me. So, in the spirit of the exhortation of the poem "As I Walked Out One Evening," let us plunge our hands in water, "up to the wrist," staring into the basin of Auden's great sequence "Sonnets from China."

II.

There is an intentional dearth of personal information in Auden's verse, especially in his early poetry. The poet was vocal in his denunciation of the cult of personality, both in the world of politics and the arts, and he resisted the cathartic allure of confession. His first book was titled *Poems*, notably demure and understated, and he frequently arranged his poems in such a way that resisted biography. Acutely aware of his own egotism and the hypnotic power of demagoguery, Auden used verse as a means of negating the impulse for self-aggrandizement by acknowledging and undermining it. As such, his poetry is often self-deprecating and full of honest appraisal, like the following excerpts taken from "Letter to Lord Byron," arguably his most biographical poem:

> The average poet by comparison
> Is unobservant, immature, lazy
>
> *
>
> All human hearts have ugly little treasures
>
> *

"I must admit that I was most precocious
(Precocious children rarely grow up good).
                    *
. . . I sign the usual pledges
To be a better poet, better man;
I'll really do it this time if I can (Auden, *Collected Poems*).

I include this obscure early poem because in my reading of Auden's *Collected Poems*, it preceded "Sonnets from China" chronologically and colored my experience of the sequence with a much-needed (at least for me) biographical sincerity. That is, after reading "Letter to Lord Byron," I felt sure the poet wasn't pulling my leg too much; that I was privileged, like a friend might be, with Auden's confidence. That may sound ridiculous, and might even be so, but to a lonely unemployed twenty-three-year-old wannabe poet, it was exactly what I needed.

I think, too, in addition to the warmth I began to feel toward the poet, my own life's circumstances colored these precious early readings and endeared Auden's work even more to me. As a recent graduate of Clemson University with a BA in English, I was understandably anxious about my future: What job prospects might a poetry enthusiast with only an undergraduate degree and a slapdash resume of restaurant positions have in the increasingly exclusive academic market? I'd been turned down for a position in every MFA program I had applied to and was nearly broke returning home from a largely frustrating few months spent working as a hostel keeper in Ireland. And so, I leaned once again on my great consolation, poetry.

I soon landed a job in a treatment center for troubled teenagers, caring for the anxious and unhappy, the manipulative and hostile, the lonely and abandoned. My days were filled with anticipatory dread as I awaited each new shift, often emerging onto the scene of a fight, an escape, or a botched suicide attempt. I walked on pins and needles with my co-workers, trying most nights just to keep the fragile peace long enough for the kids to fall asleep. In the mornings, bleary eyed from our all-night vigils, we prepared ourselves again for whatever mercurial mood the kids might be in.

In many ways I think Auden's verse record of the potential for degradation in human behavior while abroad in China mirrored in a small way my own experience working as a counselor for the dejected and violent. For Auden's great sonnet sequence, which is the subject of this book, is from beginning to end an investigation of human behavior. The circumstances of its inception seem nearly immaterial next to the broader topics unfolding in the narrative. Yes, the poem asserts that "maps can really point to places / Where life is evil now" but does so itself only sparingly, preferring instead a kind of all-encompassing, universalizing ambiguity. This allows a reader, let's say this one in particular—sitting silently with two friends at a tea shop in Asheville, N.C., reading for the first time twenty-one sonnets which would change his life—the ability to enter into what was for Auden both a highly specific encounter with suffering and a more universal firsthand experience of the ugliness of human nature.

The first half is dedicated to Auden's reimagined Adam, our Biblical progenitor and here characterized as an often pitiful and unhappy figure:

> Till, finally, there came a childish creature . . .
> Who by the gentlest wind was rudely shaken,
> Who looked for truth but always was mistaken,
> And envied his few friends . . . (128)
>   *
> He shook with hate for things he'd never seen,
> Pined for a love abstracted from its object,
> And was oppressed as he had never been. (129)
>   *
> . . . unwanted,
> Grown seedy, paunchy, pouchy, disappointed,
> He took to drink to screw his nerves to murder,
> Or sat in offices and stole,
> Boomed at his children about Law and Order,
> And hated life with heart and soul. (130)
>   *
> No more could touch the earth which he had paid for,
> Nor feel the love which he knew all about. (131)
>   *
> So an age ended, and its last deliverer died
> In bed, grown idle and unhappy . . . (132)

This universal character was someone I was intimately familiar with, both in the personal reflections on my own character defects and poor decisions, and in the fallen human figures I was faced with daily in my work. Auden personified what I saw as a quintessentially human flaw: dissatisfaction with oneself—which leads, in the end, to every human misery found in the sequence (and all those found elsewhere). And while the poems in the first half of the sequence take as their central figure the universal fallen character, the latter sonnets take on more specific questions of conflict in China and the world at large.

Knowing little of the sonnet at my initial reading, I was drawn to Auden's clever manipulation of the form to effect the highest emotional pitch correspondent to the poem's content. Taking liberties at times with line length and rhyme scheme, the poems in the latter half of the sequence, addressing the difficulties of a war-ravaged China, are often tailored to meet the needs of their specific circumstances. Whether occurring in a war room, a military hospital, a general's posh residence, or in a city square, the poems take on not only the environment but also the emotional resonance of its immediate dilemma. Auden's first of these poems (Sonnet XII)—also my favorite in the sequence—patterns this kind of syntactical immediacy best:

> Here war is harmless like a monument:
> A telephone is talking to a man;
> Flags on a map declare that troops were sent;
> A boy brings milk in bowls. There is a plan
> For living men in terror of their lives,
> Who thirst at nine who were to thirst at noon,
> Who can be lost and are, who miss their wives
> And, unlike an idea, can die too soon.
> Yet ideas can be true, although men die:
> For we have seen a myriad faces
> Ecstatic from one lie,
> And maps can really point to places
> Where life is evil now.
> Nanking. Dachau. (133)

Without spoiling too much of Dr. Levitin's analysis of the poem's first and final iteration in the latter section of this book, I'll skim briefly along its brilliant surface, emphasizing my initial impressions. These initial (and relatively ignorant) impressions illuminate an integral facet of Auden's structuring of these poems already touched upon: their immediate emotional accessibility, regardless of whatever more complex narrative meaning the lines contain.

The poem begins predictably enough, with the iambic pentameter line typical of sonnets, but halfway through begins to narrow toward its stunning conclusion (much like the narrowing of places on a map alluded to by its final stanza). This tapering to the end literally hems in both the content and the eyes to the final line: "Nanking. Dachau."—the places where life is evil now (the former a city in China infamous as a site of slaughter, the latter a Nazi concentration camp, equally infamous). As if the line itself could contain only so much horror, only the names appear, a total of four syllables coupling in a rhyme with the penultimate "Where life is evil now." The sing-song rhyme, while at risk of alienating the reader, instead draws one to the stunning power of named evil, driving home with musical intensity the gravity of its implications. My initial reading yielded only a single marginal comment: *Wow*—but the succeeding poems following suit, building on the emotional momentum of Sonnet XII in the immediacy of their painfully specific scenarios, all nearly equally bereft of marginal comments from my pen:

(Military hospital)
They are and they suffer; that is all they do:
A bandage hides the place where each is living,
His knowledge of the world restricted to
A treatment metal instruments are giving. (134)
*

(A general's mansion)
Far off, no matter what good they intended,
Two armies waited for a verbal error
With well-made implements for causing pain,
And on the issue of their charm depended
A land laid waste with all its young men slain,
Its women weeping, and its towns in terror. (135)
*

(Auden's hotel room)
When all our apparatus of report
Confirms the triumph of our enemies,
Our frontier crossed, our forces in retreat,
Violence pandemic like a new disease,
And Wrong a charmer everywhere invited . . . (137)
*

(City square)
Who needs their names? Another genus built
Those dictatorial avenues and squares,
Gigantic terraces, imposing stairs,
Men of sorry kennel, racked by guilt,
Who wanted to persist in stone for ever:
Unloved, they had to leave material traces . . . (137)
*

Each place, whether imminently dangerous, seemingly comfortable, or simply mundane, is captured by the poet in the immediate gravity of its geographic proximity to war, as well as its moral significance in the scope of conflict (both in general and in China specifically). The poems are a wonder of journalism, philosophy, political conviction, empathetic observation, and artistic craft unique to both the poet and his epoch, and unmatched in subsequent imitation since their original publication.

III.

This volume is the first I've encountered which couples a vigorous, informed close reading of a poem's text with an equally thorough analysis of the changes made (grammatical, mostly) through the process of revision, over many years, by one of the premier poetic craftsmen of our time: W. H. Auden. Initially ignorant of revision as more than just a process of "feeling out" which words or lines didn't fit the content or structure properly according to the subjective musical ear of the writer, my discovery of Dr. Levitin's dissertation (initially online, then as an eager sojourner to the archives of Columbia University's dissertation library) transformed my still amateur understanding into a more sophisticated appreciation for craft. With its meticulous attention to the ways in which even the slightest alterations in grammar can affect the semantics of a line (for instance, Auden's frequent replacement in his revisions of the definite with an indefinite article), Dr. Levitin's analysis provided me, as an established fan of Auden, with a rich source of scholarship but also with a guidebook for recognizing patterns of grammatical nuance. What might, for instance, a semicolon indicate in a line of verse as opposed to a period? Or an em dash rather than a colon? How might these seemingly slight considerations vastly alter narrative and theme? These and far more are elaborated upon in this volume.

The wonder I was swept up in as a young reader of W. H. Auden's "Sonnets from China," coupled with the discovery of Dr. Levitin's dissertation examining the poet's revision of his sequence—indeed, the discovery in the first place that the sequence had undergone so thorough a revision process—as well as my current position as an instructor of creative writing, has led me to the conviction that W. H. Auden belongs in the English classroom. And yet, in my experience, he has been frequently underutilized and underappreciated. I have my own suspicions as to why this is but largely think his neglect is due to the syntactical anomalies in his lines (grammatical constructions frequently lampooned, most famously by the poet and critic Randall Jarrell), as well as a penchant for the obscure and mythological (not to mention his later poems, inspired largely by his conversion to Christianity). But the tide is turning in his favor. As a veritable depository of verse forms and metrical experimentation, Auden's oeuvre spans the lengths and breadths of poetic construction in English from the sixteenth to the twentieth centuries. As such, it is a highly valuable tool both for aspiring and established poets, and in the cynical deprecation of form many are often confronted with in their poetic education, Auden's masterful adherence to meter and verse is a refreshing discovery.

Besides serving as valuable Auden scholarship, this present volume has the potential to transform creative writing classrooms by its meticulous, itemized analysis of poetic revision. Frequently overemphasizing content over craft, the topic of revision in classrooms has lost touch with its roots in the etymology of the word poetry itself, as a *thing made*—or in Auden's own words, *a verbal contraption.* This work seeks to correct that oversight. Dr. Levitin has examined in great detail the original sequence side-by-side with its revised counterparts, published years later (and often criticized). But far from criticizing, it is Dr. Levitin's and my conviction that Auden's growth into a craftsman of the highest order is nowhere more prominently on display than in his revision of these poems into the sequence they eventually became—the sequence which I was privileged to discover as a young man, rummaging through the archives of Columbia University, and have been equally privileged to enjoy ever since. My hope for you, dear Reader, is that you will experience that same original enjoyment, now coupled with a unique commentary offered by the book you have open before you. *Bonne journée.*

Chapter One

Introduction

The word *poet*, descending to us through Middle English, Old French, and Latin, derives from the Greek noun *poietes*, meaning maker, and ultimately from its verb *poiein*, to make, create. One of the meanings of the English word *maker*, derived from the Old English verb *macian*, now obsolete except in Scottish dialect, is poet.

That W. H. Auden thought of the poet primarily as a maker should be abundantly clear from his published statements. In the second sentence of his forward to *A Certain World,* the commonplace book that he considered "a sort of autobiography," Auden said, "A writer is a maker, not a man of action." In *About the House*, he named the poem dealing with the room in which he does his work "The Cave of Making." In his essay "Making, Knowing, Judging," originally delivered as his inaugural lecture at Oxford in June 1956, Auden praised his early master Hardy for giving him "an invaluable training in the craft of making" (Auden, *A Certain World* vii).

The material of the poet's craft is, of course, language; more concretely, words. While discussing his poetic aims in a symposium on "A Change of Air," Auden clearly acknowledged the linguistic basis of his art:

> Whatever else it may or may not be, I want every poem I write to be a hymn of praise of the English language: hence my fascination with certain speech-rhythms which can only occur in an uninflected language rich in mono-syllables, my fondness for peculiar words with no equivalents in other tongues, and my deliberate avoidance of that kind of visual imagery which has no basis in verbal experience and can therefore be translated without loss. (Auden, *The Kenyon Review* 207)

A humorous postscript might be affixed in the form of an aphorism taken from *The Dyer's Hand*: "The poet is the father of his poem; its mother is a language: one could list poems as race horses are listed out of L by P" (Auden, *The Dyer's Hand* 22).

Further evidence that Auden considered language the primary concern of the poet is provided by his homage to Dame Philology:

> A poet has to woo, not only his own Muse but also Dame Philology, and, for the beginner, the latter is the more important. As a rule, the sign that a beginner has a genuine original talent is that he is more interested in playing with words than in saying something original . . . it is only later, when he has wooed and won Dame Philology, that he can give his entire devotion to his Muse. (22)

There is also the corroboration that comes in "Making, Knowing, and Judging" where Auden stated that upon first reading a poem, though his second question is "In the broadest sense, moral," his first is technical: "Here is a verbal contraption. How does it work?" (50–51). This, then, is the question I intend to pursue in dealing with Auden's revisions.

This study is intended as an examination and analysis of the craft of poetry. Since Auden is generally acknowledged as one of the most skilled practitioners of the poet's craft writing in English, a careful study of the substantial revisions in an integrated group of his poems seemed a logical way to enter into the problems of that craft.

Concentrating on the technical or artistic significance of the revisions, I have endeavored to enumerate and classify them, show their poetic purpose, and evaluate the extent of their effectiveness. Such a detailed analysis should be of use and interest not only to students of Auden's work but also to all people concerned with or fascinated by the subtle craft of making poetry out of words.

Auden himself, in addition to numerous pronouncements about poets and poetry scattered throughout his essays, has said something about revisions. In his forward to *Collected Shorter Poems*, he succinctly outlines his method in preparing that volume. Explaining that he arranged his 1945 collection alphabetically so as not to be subject, in his late thirties, to critics' suppositions and theories about his development, he goes on to say that now he has ordered his poems chronologically, for, "Nearing sixty, I believe that I know myself and my poetic intentions better and, if anybody wants to look at my writing from an historical perspective, I have no objections." He then spoke of omissions: "Some poems which I wrote and, unfortunately, published, I have thrown out because they were dishonest, or bad-mannered, or boring" (Auden, *CSP* 15). He cited poems of egocentric youth, brashly familiar in tone, as typically bad-mannered. As for boring poems, Auden assumed that what bored him will bore us. The question of dishonesty in poems becomes so complex that I would prefer to bypass it now and consider it at length a bit later.

Auden concluded discussion of his revising procedure, saying, "On revisions as a matter of principle, I agree with Valery: 'A poem is never finished; it is only abandoned'" (15). Subtly complementing the Valery dictum is a passage from Delacroix, that appears in *The Viking Book of Aphorisms*, compiled by Auden and Louis Kronenberger: "One always has to spoil a picture a little bit, in order to finish it" (Auden and Kronenberger, *The Viking Book of Aphorisms* 293). It seems clear from these two pronouncements that, in the eyes of Valery and Delacroix, man cannot create a perfect work of art. If we turn to Auden's comment on the famous Yeats passage, "The intellect of man is forced to choose / Perfection of the life or of the work," we find that he himself seemed convinced of the ultimate imperfectability of the things of man: "This is untrue; perfection is possible in neither," was his terse response.

Valery's famous words also appear in the foreword Auden wrote for Bloomfield's *Bibliography* but qualified by the immediate rejoinder: "Yes, but it must not be abandoned too soon" (Auden, *A Bibliography)*. Here Auden indicated quite clearly that though he may believe attainment of perfection impossible, he considered striving for it of essential importance. It should come as no surprise that he, in accordance with the paradoxical logic of all life, struggled constantly toward what he knew could never be fully achieved. And in this pursuit of a perfection that can be approached but not reached, he deprived us of the luxury of resting content in the "perfection" of his past creations.

Earlier, in making clear the technical nature of my approach to Auden's revisions, I quoted briefly from his essay "Making, Knowing, and Judging," in which he speaks of a poem as "a verbal contraption." Here, in full, is the passage from which I quoted:

> Speaking for myself, the questions which interest me most when reading a poem are two. The first is technical: "Here is a verbal contraption. How does it work?" The second is, in the broadest sense, moral: "What kind of a guy inhabits this poem? What is his notion of the good life or the good place? His notion of the Evil One? What does he conceal from the reader? What does he conceal even from himself? (Auden, *The Dyer's Hand* 50–51)

This passage shows that Auden had two distinct ways of looking at a poem. The first way is to treat it as a piece of craftsmanship, a work of art, a thing unto itself. The world outside the poem is not considered. The second way is to deal with the poem as part of the world in which we all live. Not only is the outside world considered but the poem also is judged in terms of its relationship to that outside world. This second way of looking at poetry, the "moral" way, might very well prove, in the end, to be Auden's greatest strength. However, it does cause certain complications, which I must try to straighten out.

In the foreword to the Bloomfield *Bibliography*, Auden recounted in detail how he decided to throw out one of his most popular poems:

> Rereading a poem of mine, "September 1, 1939," after it had been published, I came to the line, "We must love one another or die" and said to myself: "That's a damned lie! We must die anyway." So, in the next edition, I altered it to "We must love one another and die." This didn't seem to do either, so I cut the stanza. Still no good. The whole poem, I realized, was infected with an incurable dishonesty and must be scrapped. (Auden, *A Bibliography* viii)

When he spoke of dishonesty here, Auden did not mean just an unfaithfulness to the objective "facts" of life and death but also an unfaithfulness to one's own inner truth (Even when a poem deals with the fabulous, though its outer reality may differ from ours, as long as it obeys its own laws, its inner reality must remain consistent with the writer's human experience). Therefore, when a poem speaks of the real world, it must not lie about it, either in terms of outer reality or inner. For, as Auden said in an essay on Robert Frost, "we want a poem to be true . . . to provide us with some kind of revelation about our life which will show us what life is really like and free us from self-enchantment and deception... ." This basic concern for the truth of a poem appears again when Auden discussed the response he desired from a reader: "Before he is aware of any other qualities my poem may have, I want his reaction to be: 'That's true,' or, better still, 'that's true; now, why didn't I think of it myself?'" And, in an introduction to a collection of Cavafy's poems, he says, "One duty of a poem, among others, is to bear witness to the truth" (Spears, *W.H. Auden* 189).

By and large, however, when Auden discusses honesty, he is really speaking of authenticity. Often in his revisions he seemed to be guarding himself and us from "emotional dishonesty" and other forms of personal pretense. In the foreword to *CSP*, Auden discussed this kind of personal dishonesty in poetry:

> A dishonest poem is one which expressed, no matter how well, feelings or beliefs which its author never felt or entertained. For example, I once expressed a desire for "New styles of architecture"; but I have never liked modern architecture. I prefer *old* styles, and one must be honest even about one's prejudices. Again, and much more shamefully, I once wrote: "History to the defeated / may say alas but cannot help or pardon." To say this is to equate goodness with success. It would have been bad enough if I had ever held this wicked doctrine, but

that I should have stated it simply because it sounded to me rhetorically effective is quite inexcusable. (Auden, *CSP* 15)

That Auden considered dangerous the temptation to ignore or distort one's inner truth in the service of poetic effort is further suggested by his warning in *A Certain World*: "A poet must never make a statement simply because it sounds poetically exciting; he must also believe it to be true" (Auden, *A Certain World* 425).

In his essay "Writing," Auden stated his position on the question of personal truth in poetry:

Sincerity in the proper sense of the word, meaning authenticity, is . . . or ought to be, a writer's chief preoccupation. No writer can ever judge exactly how good or bad a work of his may be, but he can always know, not immediately perhaps, but certainly in a short while, whether something he has written is authentic—in his handwriting—or a forgery.

The most painful of all experiences to a poet is to find that a poem of his which he knows to be a forgery has pleased the public and got into the anthologies. For all he knows or cares, the poem may be quite good, but that is not the point; *he* should not have written it. (Auden, *The Dyer's Hand* 18)

Auden echoed these pronouncements in discussing his jettisoned poem "September 1, 1939," in an interview: "One can never tell whether a poem one writes is good or bad. All one can tell is whether it is *you*. It may be quite a good poem, but I should never have written it." It becomes clear now that the dishonesty that disturbs him in this poem is, in fact, principally of the personal variety. Elsewhere, Auden dealt in the same terms with the extensive revisions of some of his earlier work: " . . . every poet has to ask himself what kinds of poetry, given his temperament and talent, it is authentic for him to write . . . it was not the fault of Yeats or Rilke that I allowed myself to be seduced by them into writing poems which were false to my personal poetic nature" (Auden, "Reply" 207). In all these statements, Auden manifested a belief in the basically constant nature of a man's character. Upon rereading his poems, he of course judged them by what were then his present artistic and moral standards.

A man's inner life is so complex that rarely, if ever, can he himself trace its course with certainty. Motives in the remembered past are always blurred, appearance and reality never as clearly differentiated as one would like. In revising his poetry, and attempting to prune it of dishonesty, Auden relied on the present knowledge of himself and his memory of what he was: a most difficult task.

Auden once encouraged the public's image of him as a virtuoso. However, though he may have enjoyed being a master manipulator of a "verbal contraption," he did not segregate his poetry from the moral world he inhabited. That he did not think of poetry as a pure world of its own, uncontaminated by the complexities of good and evil that are part of our daily lives, should be manifestly clear by now. A poem is definitely a "verbal contraption" and may be studied, handled, and reworked as such, but it was never, for Auden, just a "verbal contraption." It remains, always, a statement to others by an individual living in a human and moral world, a statement that ultimately must be judged by the standards of human morality. The following reflexive passage from the Postscript to "The Cave of Making" provides, in a surprisingly open manner, an added dimension to Auden's thoughts on this subject:

> You hope, yes,
>   your books will excuse you,
> save you from hell:
>   nevertheless
> without looking sad,
>   without in any way
> seeming to blame
>   (He doesn't need to,
> knowing well
>   what a lover of art
> like yourself pays heed to),
>   God may reduce you
> on Judgement Day
>   to tears of shame,
> reciting by heart
>   the poems you would
> have written, had,
>   your life been good. (Auden, *About the House* 13)

It must be said, however, that in striving for poetic perfection and for his unalloyed authentic voice, Auden did, through his extensive revisions, present the reader with some problems. For example, according to his own dictum, "if you take two poems written by the same poet at different times and you can't tell which was written first, then he's a minor poet." Assuming this to be correct, how will future readers of Auden's poetry, judging him from his revised opus, be able to find him a major poet? He will, of course, have grown as a craftsman throughout his career, but he will have obliterated the signs of his progress.

In any case, although Auden's revisions cause some confusion and some inconvenience, they signal a definite gain for the admirer of poetry. Whatever reasons may have inspired these alterations, they are now an established fact. Let us turn, then, to the revisions themselves and see if we can gain from them what Sidney maintains all poetry should provide—entertainment and instruction.

Chapter Two

London to Hongkong—A Voyage

In 1938 W. H. Auden and Christopher Isherwood, having been commissioned by Faber and Faber of London and Random House of New York to write a "travel book about the East," left for war-torn China and, after an absence of half a year, returned to England. The book they wrote about their experiences is entitled *Journey to a War*. Auden provided the sections of verse and the photographs, Isherwood the prose narrative. Auden's contribution to the volume consists of the dedicatory sonnet to E. M. Forster; a section entitled "London to Hongkong," containing an introductory poem, "The Voyage," "Macao," and "Hongkong," documenting stations along their way; and, following the body of the prose narrative and the accompanying photographs, a section entitled "In Time of War," composed of a sequence of twenty-seven sonnets followed by a verse commentary of twelve pages.

The fate of these poems can be easily summarized. "In Time of War," the sonnet sequence with a verse commentary, now appears in Auden's personally edited *Collected Shorter Poems, 1927–1957*, "Sonnets from China." The verse commentary has been discarded as have six of the twenty-seven sonnets originally comprising the sequence.

My analysis of these poems follows the order of their appearance in *CSP*. Preceding each discussion will be the text of the original and revised versions of the poem in question. When a poem from *Journey to a War* is omitted, I present the original text and briefly try to account for its elimination. Whenever the order of the poems differs from that found in the original, I will point out the change and offer an explanation. Since the dedicatory poem to E. M. Forster now appears as the concluding poem of the sequence "Sonnets from China," I leave it for later and instead turn immediately to the opening section of *Journey to a War*, "London to Hongkong."

The first change one notices is in the title. The new sequence discards "London to Hongkong" as its title, adopting and adapting instead the original title of the sequence's introductory poem, "The Voyage." The definite article is dropped in favor of the humbler indefinite article which, limiting the substantive, brings the title firmly down to earth. "A Voyage" is smaller, more ordinary, more tangible, more real than its Platonic predecessor. Yet, while the change in article limits, localizes, and makes concrete, the noun itself retains echoes of universality. Auden demonstrates in this retitling one of his greatest concerns—the desire to reduce to size his images, while at the same time retaining their larger, more abstract suggestions. We will see, throughout this study, how Auden tends to eliminate the definite article whenever he conveniently can, apparently feeling that in his more dogmatic, didactic days he used it too freely to give his work a facile strength, assurance, and universality. Referring briefly but pointedly to his former customary practice in this matter, Auden says in the foreword to *CSP*: "Re-reading my poems, I find that in the nineteen-thirties I fell into some very slovenly verbal habits. The definite article is always a headache in English, but my addiction to German usage became a disease" (Auden, *CSP* 16). It will become clear that revision has swept away almost all sign of that disease.

The Voyage (*Journey to a War*)

Where does the journey look which the watcher upon the quay,
Standing under his evil star, so bitterly envies?
When the mountains swim away with slow calm strokes, and the gulls
Abandon their vow? Does it still promise the Juster Life?

And, alone with his heart at last, does the traveler find
In the vaguer touch of the wind and the fickle flash of the sea
Proofs that somewhere there exists, really, the Good Place,
As certain as those the children find in stones and holes?

No, he discovers nothing; he does not want to arrive.
The journey is false; the false journey really an illness
On the false island where the heart cannot act and will not suffer:
He condones the fever; he is weaker than he thought; his weakness
      is real.

But at moments, as when the real dolphins with leap and abandon
Cajole for recognition, or, far away, a real island
Gets up to catch his eye, the trance is broken: he remembers
The hours, the places where he was well; he believes in joy.

And maybe the fever shall have a cure, the true journey an end
Where hearts meet and are really true: and away this sea that parts
The hearts that alter, but is the same, always; and goes
Everywhere, joining the false and the true, but cannot suffer.
(Auden, *Journey* 11)

Whither? (*Collected Shorter Poems*)

Where does this journey look which the watcher upon the quay,
Standing under his evil star, so bitterly envies,
As the mountains swim away with slow calm strokes
And the gulls abandon their vow? Does it promise a Juster Life?

Alone with his heart at last, does the fortunate traveler find
In the vague touch of a breeze, the fickle flash of a wave,
Proofs that somewhere exists, really, the Good Place,
Convincing as those that children find in stones and holes?

No, he discovers nothing: he does not want to arrive.
His journey is false, his unreal excitement really an illness
On a false island where the heart cannot act and will not suffer:
He condones his fever; he is weaker than he thought; his weakness
    is real.

But at moments, as when real dolphins with leap and panache
Cajole for recognition or, far away, a real island
Gets up to catch his eye, his trance is broken: he remembers
Times and places where he was well; he believes in joy,

That, maybe, his fever shall find a cure, the true journey and an end
Where hearts meet and are really true, and crossed this ocean, that
    parts
Hearts which alter but is the same always, that goes
Everywhere, as truth and falsehood go, but cannot suffer. (Auden,
CSP 119)

The revised introductory poem, having given its title, rearticled, to the sequence as a whole, is now provided with the new title, "Whither?" Clearly posing the question that all voyages evoke, it also indicates that Auden, in spite of his intense partiality for the indefinite article, does not intend to abandon the universal implications of his image. One might note that the relative archaism of the locution implies a timelessness in the question and, perhaps, in the answer as well.

"Whither?" is an exercise in accentual verse. Each line of the five quatrains contains anywhere from eleven to eighteen syllables, but there are always six major accents to a line. A caesura divides each line roughly in half and usually the accents are evenly distributed on either side of it. A comparison of the shortest and the longest lines reveals, in spite of their evident disparity, a basic accentual conformity (in lieu of accent marks, the stressed syllables/words have been bolded):

> As the **mountains swim away** with **slow calm strokes**
> He con**dones** his **fever**; he is **weak**er than he **thought**; his **weak**ness
> is **real**

There is considerable alliteration through this poem, particularly in the first two stanzas, but it does not appear in the regular patterns characteristics of Anglo-Saxon alliterative verse. In the first three lines of the poem there is prominent alliteration that seems determined by strict rules:

> Where does this journey look which the watcher upon the quay,
> Standing under his evil star, so bitterly envies,
> As the mountains swim away with slow calm strokes

Yet the fourth line of this quatrain contains no true alliteration. The four lines of the next quatrain vary remarkably, the first having two alliterative couples, one on each side of the caesura, "Alone with his heart at last, does the fortunate traveler find," the second only one alliterative effect, "fickle flash," and the third its alliterating words at the extremes, rather too distant to resound together significantly, "Proofs that somewhere exists, really, the Good Place." There is no alliteration in the fourth line at all.

We have, then, a poem of five quatrains characterized by six stress lines divided roughly in half by a caesura, with occasional, unsystematic, alliterative effects.

"Whither?" deals with the fact that most voyages do not lead to the Good Place, nor are expected to, and that the traveler actually, though unwillingly, knows his journey to be false and pointless. Yet there are moments "as when real dolphins with leap and panache / Cajole for recognition" when he does awaken to a forgotten reality of joy and health and believes that perhaps the journey can end "Where hearts meet and are really true," and that the ocean which never changes and "cannot suffer," the ocean of life, presumably, may perhaps be happily crossed after all.

"The Voyage" undergoes numerous minor changes in becoming "Whither?" The most prevalent is the omission of the definite article. I have already pointed out that the title of this poem is now affixed to the group as a whole, but with the indefinite article replacing the definite. In the poem itself there are no less than seventeen definite articles eliminated, a remarkable number for a poem of only twenty lines. Often "the" is replaced by a more precise modifier such as "this," in line one, or "his" (referring to the voyager), twice in line ten and once in lines twelve, fifteen, and seventeen. Sometimes, when convenient, the definite article is simply omitted as in lines thirteen, sixteen (twice), nineteen and twenty (twice). The indefinite article replaces the definite four times, in lines four, six (twice), and eleven. Once the relative pronoun "that," its use optional in context, is inserted to fill in rhythmically for an eliminated "the."

What is the effect of all this? By eliminating the definite article, Auden achieves a fresh sense of reality. In place of abstraction he gives us things that are specific, particular, discrete, concrete, precise, and local. "His journey is false" is both more limited and more palpable than "The journey is false." It seems more factual, less pontifical.

We can learn more from a consideration of changes involving both article and noun. For example, line four originally concluded: "Does it still promise the Juster Life? This now reads: "Does it promise a juster life?" The conversion of definite to indefinite article is matched by the conversion of upper to lower case. The universal, the Platonic, dogmatically assumed in the earlier version, becomes the human, limited, and in its modesty, the possible.

Movement away from the general and the abstract toward the particular and the concrete is well illustrated by changes in line six: "In the vaguer touch of the wind and the fickle flash of the sea" becomes "In the vague touch of a breeze, the fickle flash of a wave." Not only have two definite articles been replaced by indefinite ones, but the nouns have been significantly altered from unevocative or even misleading ones to others more meaningful because more precise and accurate. The touch of a breeze may very well be vague, that of a wind hardly. As for the flash of the sea, it is actually the wave in the sea that moves and flashes, and Auden's revision centers attention upon the actual moving thing itself, the particular, instead of the vast and general, ultimately intangible, sea. We may note in passing that the comparative "vaguer" had been used most vaguely, it being impossible to determine what the wind was *vaguer* than; its replacement by the simple form "vague" ends all confusion.

Several other minor changes are worth mentioning. An unnecessary "and" at the start of the second stanza is eliminated, as is a superfluous "there" in line seven. In line ten overly heavy repetition is pared down: "The journey is false; the false journey really an illness" (followed in line eleven by "On the false island . . . ") is changed to "His journey is false, his unreal excitement really an illness" (followed now by "On a false island"). In line sixteen "The hours, the places" becomes "Times and places": two definite articles are swiftly dispatched, the naked nouns are now equal in abstraction, and balance and parallel structure have been served. The change from "abandon" to "panache" in the fourth stanza makes the leaping dolphins more dandyish, more sophisticated, perhaps even lighter. The somewhat frivolous flavor that the word carries with it in this context seems appropriate enough but is a flavor which Auden may have been unwilling or unable to introduce in his graver, more didactic days.

The changes in the last three lines of the poem are fairly substantial: "and away this sea" becomes "and crossed this ocean," a more accurate description of the hoped-for resolution to life's fever, to our false journey, for though the illusion may be swept away, the sea or ocean, our life, is real and, one way or another, must be crossed. In the last line of the poem Auden originally had spoken of the sea which goes "Everywhere, joining the false and the true, but cannot suffer," but he now revises this description to a more precise formulation, speaking of an ocean that goes "Everywhere, as truth and falsehood go, but cannot suffer." Apparently, Auden felt that "joining" was open to ambiguous interpretation, perhaps involving the suggestion that true and false are all the same. This possible misunderstanding is avoided by the new version which makes clear that both truth and falsehood are everywhere, without ever implying that they are indissolubly intermixed. In the process of revising this line, Auden has, we may note, extirpated two more "the"s.

Another type of alteration that Auden introduces fairly extensively in his revising involves the intensified use of verbs and verbals. In this poem there are two examples of verbals replacing prepositional or adjectival constructions. "As certain as" becomes "convincingly as," while the awkward, elliptical " . . . and away this sea that parts" becomes " . . . and crossed this sea that parts." In the first phrase the intent seems to be to sharpen the effect of the expression by replacing a daily locution, used in countless folksy idiomatic sayings, with a somewhat more substantial sounding word, a word that may still retain some of the strength that it has as a transitive verb (a similar revision occurs later in "A Major Port," the locution "Nothing is certain" being replaced by the sharp image and sound of "No data." In the second phrase, as already noted, the meaning is made considerably clearer by the revision.

One last revision involving a verb appears in this poem. As he does regularly in reworking the poems from *Journey to a War*, Auden replaces a static verb, in this case *to have*, with an active verb: "And maybe the fever shall have a cure . . . " becomes "That, maybe, his fever shall find a cure... ." In the earlier version the line gives a passive impression because the verb does nothing to imply volition, striving, or motion, whereas in the revised line the verb implies that the illness seeks its own cure and that, by extension, the traveler who has the fever is himself actively seeking, or at least hoping for, some salvation.

As we continue to examine Auden's revisions in other poems we will come across many of the same characteristic concerns that we have encountered here: a passion for eliminating youthful, arrogant, didactic definite articles; a sustained interest in increasing specificity and concretion of image; a movement toward the actual, or particular, and away from the abstract; a greater attention to correctness of expression, to accuracy within the rhetorical form; and finally a desire to enliven and freshen the imagery through a careful selection of verbs and verbals.

The Ship (*Journey to a War*)

The streets are brightly lit; our city is kept clean:
The third class have the greasiest cards, the first play high;
The beggars sleeping in the bows have never seen
What can be done in staterooms; no one asks why.

Lovers are writing letters, sportsmen playing ball;
One doubts the honour, one the beauty, of his wife;
A boy's ambitious; perhaps the captain hates us all;
Someone perhaps is leading the civilized life.

It is our culture that with such calm progresses
Over the barren plains of a sea; somewhere ahead
The septic East, a war, new flowers and new dresses.

Somewhere a strange and shrewd To-morrow goes to bed
Planning the test for men from Europe; no one guesses
Who will be most ashamed, who richer, and who dead. (Auden, *Journey* 12)

The Ship (*Collected Shorter Poems*)

All streets are brightly lit; our city is kept clean;
Her Third-Class deal from greasy packs, her First bid high;
Her beggars banished to the bows have never seen
What can be done in state-rooms: no one asks why.

> Lovers are writing letters, athletes playing ball,
> One doubts the virtue, one the beauty of his wife,
> A boy's ambitious: perhaps the captain hates us all;
> Someone perhaps is leading a civilized life.

> Slowly our Western culture in full pomp progresses
> Over the barren plains of a sea; somewhere ahead
> A septic East, odd fowl and flowers, odder dresses:

> Somewhere a strange and shrewd To-morrow goes to bed,
> Planning a test for men from Europe; no one guesses
> Who will be most ashamed, who richer, and who dead. (Auden, *CSP*
> 119–20)

In *Journey to a War*, "The Voyage" is followed by "The Sphinx" and "The Ship," but in *CSP* their order is reversed, resulting in a more logical development in which first the ship carrying the Europeans to the East is described, and then the first sentinel of another world is encountered.

"The Ship" is a modified Petrarchan sonnet with a rhyme scheme of ABAB CDCD EFE FEF. Its lines, in iambic hexameter, are longer than the standard iambic pentameter line characteristic of the sonnets from *Journey to a War*, allowing more room for descriptive amplification.

"The Ship" deals with a microcosmic Western Civilization moving toward an encounter with the East, the unknown, quite unaware of the tests, trials, sufferings, and embarrassments, not to mention failures, that await it.

Comparing texts, one immediately discovers again a fastidious omission or conversion of the definite article. Eight definite articles are eliminated, five in the first three lines. Three are replaced by the indefinite article, three by the pronoun *her* (referring to the ship), one is simply dropped, and, in the first line of the poem, "The streets" becomes the more defined "All streets."

Several lines have undergone major revisions. In describing the ship's occupants, Auden originally wrote:

> The third class have the greasiest cards, the first play high;
> The beggars sleeping in the bows have never seen
> What can be done in staterooms; no one asks why.

The first line and a half have been changed, becoming, "Her Third-Class deal from greasy packs, her First bid high; / Her beggars banished to the bows... ." Not only do we find an efficient elimination of definite articles, but we also find a crisper line, freed from the rather awkward sounding "greasiest," enlivened by an active, particularizing verb which shows the greasy pack in action instead of simply there. This salutary change from the possessive, static verb *to have* to the active verb *to deal*, is similar to the change in "Whither?" from "And maybe the fever shall have a cure . . . " to "That, maybe, his fever shall find a cure... ." This is not the only revision of a verb in these lines, however. "Play" is replaced by "bid," a definite improvement in terms of accuracy or clarity, for one can, if one chooses and dares, bid high, but it remains a bit obscure what playing high might mean. Of course, the implication remains the same—the first-class passengers can afford to bid high, to go for the big win, because they know that they are winners even if they lose the hand—they are the successful, the self-assured. In the next line the present participle "sleeping" is replaced by the past participle "banished." A serious shift has taken place for now the emphasis is not on what the beggars are doing (sleeping) but on what has been done to them (banished). They are now the objects of an action (not grammatically, but in effect, as the past participle is a kind of elliptical passive construction) and are seen to be both passive and impotent. In the process of changing the verbal Auden has augmented the alliterative effect already established by "beggars . . . in the bows."

Two more lines are substantially revised in the new version of "The Ship." After having described the occupants of the vessel in the octave, Auden originally begins the sestet with "It is our culture that with such calm progresses," but has now modified this to read "Slowly our Western culture in full pomp progresses." Clearly this latter version says more about the nature of our culture. Whereas the earlier version wastes half the line proclaiming what the ship symbolizes, the revised line assumes we see the ship as a microcosm of our Western culture, and so proceeds immediately to delineate it, the "Slowly . . . in full pomp" telling of a self-assured stateliness in which "no one guesses" what will come. The revised line, by speaking of "Western culture" presents us with a pointed contrast, perhaps too pointed, to "A septic East."

The last extensive change in this poem occurs in line eleven. We were originally told that what lies ahead for the traveler is "The septic East, a war, new flowers and new dresses." I assume that reference to the war is deleted because, though it was of topical value in the context of *Journey to a War*, it would now appear foolishly dated, especially since we all know that, shortly after the poem was written, war was raging in Europe and could no longer be identified merely with the "septic East." As for the shift from newness to oddness, it seems that Auden wishes to emphasize the strangeness, the unknown quality, of the newness. "Odd" prepares us for "a strange and shrewd To-morrow" of which "no one guesses" the outcome. So we have alliterating elements of natural daily existence, "fowl and flowers," and artifacts of daily human existence, man-made dresses, awaiting the travelers in a "septic East," but all things, those natural and those artificial, that await them, are odd, strange, unknown.

There remain only two minor word changes to mention. In the first line of the second stanza "sportsman" becomes "athletes." Besides its Greek meaning of competitor, "athlete" carried with it more physical overtones than its synonym. In any case it adds an alliterative l to "Lovers are writing letters." In the next line Auden replaces "honour" with "virtue," for, as he says, "When a husband suspects that his wife has been unfaithful to him, it is her virtue that he doubts. If anyone's honor is tarnished, it is his."

As in "Whither?" there are a number of relatively unimportant punctuation changes involving exchanges of colons and semicolons for each other. However, one punctuation change of significance occurs in the revised eleventh line, which, instead of ending in a period, now ends in a colon, effectively intensifying the link between "odd fowl and flowers, odder dresses" and the next stanza's "Strange and shrewd To-morrow."

The Sphinx (*Journey to a War*)

Did it once issue from the carver's hand
Healthy? Even the earliest conquerors saw
The face of a slick ape, a bandaged paw,
A Presence in the hot invaded land.

The lion of a tortured stubborn star,
It does not like the young, nor love, nor learning:
Time hurt it like a person; it lies, turning
A vast behind on shrill America,

And witnesses. The huge hurt face accuses,
And pardons nothing, least of all success.
The answers that it utters have no uses

To those who face akimbo its distress:
"Do people like me?" *No.* The slave amuses
The lion. "Am I to suffer always? *Yes.* (Auden, *Journey* 12–13)

The Sphinx (*Collected Shorter Poems*)

Did it once issue from the carver's hand
Healthy? Even the earliest conqueror saw
The face of a sick ape, a bandaged paw,
An ailing lion crouched on dirty sand.

We gape, then go uneasily away:
It does not like the young nor love learning.
Time hurt it like a person: it lies turning
A vast behind on shrill America,

And witnesses. The huge hurt face accuses
And pardons nothing, least of all success:
What counsel it might offer it refuses
To those who face akimbo its distress.

"Do people like me?" *No.* The slave amuses
The lion. "Am I to suffer always?" *Yes.* (Auden, *CSP* 120)

"The Sphinx," which in *CSP* follows "The Ship," originally appeared as a modified Petrarchan sonnet rhyming ABBA CDDC EFE FEF. In its revised form, three lines have been entirely rewritten, and the final tercets have been converted into a quatrain and a couplet by the shifting of the first line of the last stanza to the end of the penultimate stanza, giving the poem the structure of a Shakespearean sonnet. The meter is basically iambic pentameter, as it is in most of the sonnets in *Journey to a War*. Those lines ending with a feminine rhyme contain a characteristic eleventh syllable.

The poem presents the Sphinx as a maimed, unhealthy and unhappy omen; an accuser of facilely optimistic human achievers; an inscrutable, suffering lion that refuses to allow us to continue to deny grim reality. "The Sphinx" picks up the question of truth and falsehood that was raised in "Whither?" while elaborating upon the conflict between West and East that was suggested in "The Ship." The Sphinx, clearly associated with ancient cultures and the East, is, of course, antithetical to the brash and optimistic technological culture of America and the West. Much of the sonnet's imagery can be traced to the impressionistic travel essay "Escales," which was published before "The Sphinx" was written:

There it lies, in the utter stillness of its mortal injuries; the flat oval face of a scarred and blinded baboon . . . no longer a statue but a living, changing creature of stone . . . its paws clumsily bandaged with bricks . . . asking no riddle, turning

its back upon America—injured baboon with a lion's cruel mouth, in the middle
of invaded Egypt. (Isherwood, "Escales" *Exhumations* 145)

There are three major alterations in this poem but scarcely any minor ones.
In the earlier version Auden, in describing how the Sphinx must have looked
even to early conquerors, refers to it as "A Presence in the hot invaded land."
This line has been entirely rewritten to read, "An ailing lion crouched on
dirty sand." Characteristically, Auden has eliminated the capitalized abstraction, putting in its place a diminished metaphoric creature of wounded flesh
that elicits from the reader a strange mixture of pity and fear. No longer a
"Presence," and deprived of that heroically abstract setting, a romantic "hot,
invaded land," the "ailing lion" suffers now in a shabby reality of "dirty
sand." Abstract creature and abstract place have given way to a sad, disturbing, earthbound image. The addition of the verbal "crouched," shaping the
creature in his ugly setting before us, intensifies, ambiguously, both our pity
and our fear.

The first line of the second stanza is completely changed. Probably Auden
felt that the revised final line of the previous stanza made superfluous "The
lion of a tortured stubborn star." In any case it seems clear that he was eager
to banish his very un-American rhyme of "star" with "America," preferring
the head rhyme of "away-America." The focus of the line, after revision,
shifts from the Sphinx to us: "We gape, then go uneasily away," showing our
ultimate incapacity to cope with the Sphinx and the truth of its forlorn, yet
pitiless gaze. What we value—youth, love, learning—has no impact on it. But
time, the element in which we live and which we fear, does affect the stone
lion: "Time hurt it like a person." And, reminded of our mortality, we move
uneasily away. It should be noted that again Auden has revitalized a line with
a well-chosen verb, this time the dramatic *gape*. The other verb in the revised
line, *go away*, I find rather weak. It seems that Auden relies, in this case, on
his adverb to carry the weight of suggestion.

The third line of the third stanza has been changed from "The answers
that it utters have no uses" to "What counsel it might offer it refuses." Since
the Sphinx, though it may influence one's thoughts, does not literally speak,
Auden sensibly drops the verb "utter," which always implies actual vocaliza-
tion, at the same time shifting to the conditional tense, thereby making the
Sphinx's pronouncements only a possibility and, as it turns out, a possibility
denied. The change in the line's end word from "uses" to "refuses" replaces
a near rhyme for "accuses" and "amuses" with a full rhyme. This type of
revision occurs several times in later sonnets and is explained by Auden's
comment in the foreword to *CSP*:

I . . . find that my ear will no longer tolerate rhyming a voiced *S* with an unvoiced. I have had to leave a few such rhymes because I cannot at the moment see a way to get rid of them, but I promise not to do it again. (Auden, *CSP* 16)

The final change of importance in this poem is the conversion of the two tercets to quatrain and couplet. The change is beneficial, I feel, since the two short questions and the two monosyllabic, cold-blooded, dispassionate answers stand out more starkly and effectively in the couplet. The confrontation between man's timorous hopes and anxieties and unpitying reality is sharply delineated:

> "Do people like me?" *No.* The slave amuses
> The lion. "Am I to suffer always?" *Yes.*

Note that the Sphinx's reply, originally in no way set off from the narrative, now appears not in quotes but in italics, probably as an indication that the words are unspoken.

There are nine punctuation changes in this poem. Several commas are omitted, colons are interchanged with periods, and one semicolon becomes a colon. None of these changes seems of great significance. One might note, however, a tendency throughout Auden's revising to eliminate superfluous commas.

The Traveller (*Journey to a War*)

> Holding the distance up before his face
> And standing under the peculiar tree,
> He seeks the hostile unfamiliar place,
> It is the strangeness that he tries to see
>
> Of lands where he will not be asked to stay;
> And fights with all his power to be the same,
> The One who loves Another far away,
> And has a home, and wears his father's name.
>
> Yet he and his are always the Expected:
> The harbours touch him as he leaves the steamer,
> The Soft, the Sweet, the Easily-Accepted;
> The cities hold his feeling like a fan;
> And crowds make room for him without a murmur,
> As the earth has patience with the life of man. (Auden, *Journey* 13)

The fourth poem appearing in the "London to Hongkong" section of *Journey to a War* is "The Traveller." Auden has chosen to omit it entirely from *CSP*. No doubt the plethora of capitalized abstractions (six) and of the definite articles (fifteen) vexed him, but more importantly, he may have found the poem inappropriately personal. Though Auden discusses omissions in the forewords to both *CSP* and Bloomfield's *Bibliography*, nowhere does he comment on individual omissions from *Journey to a War*. I myself am not always sure why Auden has discarded a particular poem, though I try to account for his decision in each case. In his dissertation variorum to Auden's *CSP* and *Collected Longer Poems*, William Quesenbery, remarking on the elimination of "The Traveller" along with six other sonnets from "In Time of War," theorizes:

> Auden may have dropped all seven of the poems simply because he felt that he could reduce the number of poems selected from this volume without seri-ously affecting its structure, particularly the structure of the "In Time of War" section. He might readily have regarded twenty-nine poems, one long poem and twenty-eight sonnets (this refers only to "In Time of War") as a dispro-portionate representation for one volume. Alternatively or additionally, he may have thought the total number of sonnets in *CSP* disproportionately high (Quesenbery, "Variant Readings in W.H. Auden's Poetry" 94).

These suggestions, though useful in a general way, leave open of course the difficult question of why individual sonnets are cut.

"Macao" and "Hongkong," the last two sonnets in this section of *Journey to a War*, appear in reverse order in *CSP*, and then are followed by a final poem entitled "A Major Port," a poem which had originally been sonnet XXV in the sonnet sequence "In Time of War."

Hongkong (*Journey to a War*)

The leading characters are wise and witty;
Substantial men of birth and education
With wide experience of administration,
They know the manners of a modern city.

Only servants enter unexpected;
Their silence has a fresh dramatic use:
Here in the East the bankers have erected
A worthy temple to the Comic Muse.

Ten thousand miles from home and What's-her-name,
The bugle on the Late Victorian hill
Puts out the soldier's light; off-stage, a war

Thuds like the slamming of a distant door:
We cannot postulate a General Will;
For what we are, we have ourselves to blame. (Auden, *Journey* 13)

Hong Kong (*CSP*)

Its leading characters are wise and witty,
Their suits well-tailored, and they wear them well,
Have many a polished parable to tell
About the *mores* of a trading city.

Only the servants enter unexpected,
Their silent movements make dramatic news;
Here in the East our bankers have erected
A worthy temple to the Comic Muse.

Ten thousand miles from home and What's-Her-Name
A bugle on this Late Victorian hill
Puts out the soldier's light; off-stage, a war

Thuds like the slamming of a distant door:
Each has his comic role in life to fill,
Though Life be neither comic nor a game. (Auden, *CSP* 120–21)

"Hong Kong" is another sonnet in iambic pentameter with a rhyme scheme of ABBA CDCD EFG GFE. Its use of two different rhyme patterns in the quatrains is the first instance of what, in the poems from *Journey to a War*, is a rare practice. Though the two sonnets which follow "Hong Kong" in *CSP* both exhibit similar combinations—"Macao" reversing the order to ABAB CDDC, "A Major Port" returning to ABBA CDCD—none of the poems from "In Time of War" preserved in "Sonnets from China" shows such atypical patterning. Only the dedicatory poem "To E.M. Forster," placed at the end of "Sonnets from China," now, in its revised form, unexpectedly displays in its octave a pattern identical to that of "Hong Kong."

Six of the lines in the "Hong Kong" octave originally ended in feminine rhymes, but revision replaces "administration-education" with the simple masculine rhyme, "well-tell." The only masculine rhyming pair in the original octave was the amusing disyllabic rhyme of "dramatic use" with "Comic Muse." In the sestet, all endings form perfect masculine rhymes. Throughout the poem, all lines with feminine endings have eleven syllables and all with masculine have ten, except for the revised third line, which has one extra syllable.

The poem deals with the nature of this city and those who run it: sophisticated, cultured, worldly men who forge the kind of life they want and deftly maintain it. These "leading characters" are matched by the Catholic and European in "Macao," both producing cities of secular success (for themselves), but cities without greatness or spirituality, in which "nothing serious can happen" and in which "each has his comic role to fill."

"Hong Kong" is both descriptive and didactic, and the changes that Auden has made affect both aspects of the poem. The body of the sonnet describes, and the final two lines reflect upon what has been described.

The first stanza is almost completely changed in the course of revision:

> The leading characters are wise and witty;
> Substantial men of birth and education
> With wide experience of administration,
> They know the manners of a modern city.

Becomes:

> Its leading characters are wise and witty,
> Their suits well-tailored, and they wear them well,
> Have many a polished parable to tell
> About the *mores* of a trading city.

Instead of telling us what these men are like, Auden shows us how they look, how they dress, and tells us something of their conversation. In line two he presents us with specific details ("suits well-tailored") and social judgment ("they wear them well"), while at the same time managing to add three alliterating *w*'s to echo the first line's "wise and witty." In the following two lines, through careful selection of language, he gives us a taste of their savoir-faire and general sophistication. By calling their stories "polished parables," he implies the elegant cultivation of these men and their consummate knowledge of how things stand in their world. They understand so thoroughly "the *mores* of a trading city" that they can present quintessential truths through parables. The modifier, urbane and gaily alliterative, conflicts meanwhile with the unavoidable biblical associations of the noun, thus preparing us, in a way, for the chilling summation of the gravely serious last two lines. By italicizing *mores*, Auden calls attention to its Latin origin, further emphasizing the urbanity of Hong Kong's "leading characters."

As a result of this extensive revising, now, instead of merely knowing something about these men, we can, seeing and hearing them, actually feel their presence.

In the second stanza the second line is recast from "Their silence has a fresh dramatic use" to "Their silent movements make dramatic news." The earlier version remains obscure to me, the word "use" in particular seeming out of place. In any case, the replacement of "use" by "news," similar to that of "uses" by "refuses" in "The Sphinx," converts a near to a full rhyme. The meaning in the revised line is clear enough: Everything in their city is so completely controlled by the leading characters that the only dramatic news is the silent entrance of occasional servants, "unexpected" not to their master but to the outside observer.

Before moving on to the sestet, the elimination of the definite article is worth mentioning, for although in this poem only three examples occur, one of them is of some importance. Relatively uninteresting are the changes in the first stanza from "the leading characters" to "its leading characters" and in the third stanza from "the Late Victorian hill" to "this late Victorian hill." However, in the second stanza "the bankers" have become "our bankers," making clear that the founders of the "temple to the Comic Muse" are invaders, westerners, Europeans, and that the onus of Hong Kong's thoroughly worldly existence falls upon western shoulders. The conflict between East and West, most clearly suggested in the third stanza of "The Ship," is again evoked by the provocative juxtaposition in this revised line of "the East" and "our bankers."

We should not forget "A worthy temple to the Comic Muse" for in thoroughly revising the final two lines of the poem, Auden concentrates upon elaborating the idea of life in Hong Kong as comic. The didacticism of "We cannot postulate a General Will; / For what we are, we have ourselves to blame" has become something quite different, something less dogmatic and declamatory, but in its quiet undercutting of all that precedes it, subtly ominous: "Each has his comic role in life to fill, / Though Life is neither comic nor a game." The simple statement of the last line casts a threatening cloud over a world in which facility and elegance, reflected in such rhymes as "witty-city" have held happy sway. The deliberate capitalization of "Life" in the last line indicates a contrast with the lower case "life" in the penultimate line. The implication is clear: on the small field of *life* within Hong Kong, the thud of a war off-stage is ignored, and only comic roles are played, but at the same time *Life* marches on, "neither comic nor a game," though "our bankers" with their "polished parables" and "temple to the Comic Muse" have established an entirely worldly city, neither a City of Justice nor of Love. The imagery, whether biblical or classical, is gravely ironic, for in this city only Mammon is being served.

It seems to me that through these major changes the poem is significantly strengthened. We now have numerous specific details to visualize and from which to build up a living reality, a strange and fertile juxtaposition to ponder ("polished parables"), and a powerful, undeclamatory, grave conclusion.

Macao (*Journey to a War*)

A weed from Catholic Europe, it took root
Between the yellow mountains and the sea,
And bore these gay stone houses like a fruit,
And grew on China imperceptibly.

Rococo images of Saint and Saviour
Promise her gamblers fortunes when they die;
Churches beside the brothels testify
That faith can pardon natural behavior.

This city of indulgence need not fear
The major sins by which the heart is killed,
And governments and men are torn to pieces:

Religious clocks will strike; the childish vices
Will safeguard the low virtues of the child;
And nothing serious can happen here. (Auden, *Journey* 13–14)

Macao (*CSP*)

A weed from Catholic Europe, it took root
Between some yellow mountains and a sea,
Its gay stone houses an exotic fruit,
A Portugal-cum-China oddity.

Rococo images of Saint and Saviour
Promise its gamblers fortunes when they die,
Churches alongside brothels testify
That faith can pardon natural behavior.

A town of such indulgence need not fear
Those mortal sins by which the strong are killed
And limbs and governments are torn to pieces:

Religious clocks will strike, the childish vices
Will safeguard the low virtues of the child,
And nothing serious can happen here. (Auden, *CSP* 121)

"Macao" is a modified Petrarchan sonnet in regular iambic pentameter. Its lines with masculine endings consist of ten syllables, those with feminine eleven. It has an atypical rhyme scheme of ABAB CDDC EFG GFE, reversing the pattern of the quatrains found in "Hong Kong." "Macao" introduces two consonantal rhyming pairs in its tercets, "killed-child" and "pieces-vices," surrounding them by a perfect rhyme in the first and last lines of the sestet, "fear-here."

This companion piece to "Hong Kong" describes the tiny thriving Portuguese colony of Macao, nestled on the periphery of China. It is a European-Asian Catholic enclave, a potpourri of religion and vice where "childish vices / Will safeguard the low virtues of the child, / And nothing serious can happen... ."

The first stanza undergoes some major revising. The second line merely gives up two definite articles, but the next two lines are completely rewritten: "And bore these gay stone houses like a fruit, / And grew on China imperceptibly" becomes "Its gay stone houses an exotic fruit, / A Portugal-cum-China oddity." In making these changes Auden has uncharacteristically sacrificed two verbs, "bore" and "grew," apparently feeling that the metaphor of the weed is clear enough without their support. Though the metaphor holds, I find the original lines more effective visually because of their verbs. Revision has also eliminated the initial "and" in each line, a device Auden used a great deal in the poems in *Journey to a War* as a link between descriptive clauses. His desire to do away with this repetitious incantatory linking word is even clearer in the revised sonnet sequence "Sonnets from China," particularly in sonnet VIII where eleven *and*'s are eliminated, nine of them in the initial position of their line.

In the revised lines the "gay stone houses" remain a fruit, but now the fruit is exotic and metaphoric, whereas before it was unmodified and the vehicle of a simile. The last line of the stanza in its earlier form conveyed a sense of the city's slow yet unrelenting growth, but now, deprived of its verb, it instead succinctly presents the strangeness of Macao's makeup in terms of its mixed heritage.

Alterations in the second stanza are slight. "Her gamblers" becomes "its gamblers," a semicolon becomes a comma (this change occurs twice more, both times in the last stanza of the poem), and "Churches beside the brothels testify" becomes "Churches alongside brothels testify," a definite article being eliminated, an alliterative effect of questionable worth cancelled, and the rhythm of the line made more fluid by the trisyllabic word. One could also argue that whatever ambiguity "beside" allowed (being read to mean *as well as*) has been eliminated by the change.

The third stanza has undergone extensive revision:

> This city of indulgence need not fear
> The major sins by which the heart is killed,
> And governments and men are torn to pieces

Becomes:

> A town of such indulgence need not fear
> Those mortal sins by which the strong are killed
> And limbs and governments are torn to pieces

Perhaps the city gives way to the town because the latter is an earlier stage of growth, a less mature and fully formed stage, therefore more appropriate for Macao, a place where "nothing serious can happen," a place basically of children who "need not fear . . . mortal sins," a place where responsibility and guilt seem alien things.

The revised second line seems to reflect a change in attitude. When the original version speaks of "major sins" it looks as if Auden is going out of his way to avoid using a standard, common, Christian term, integral to western literature and thought, that would leave the stain of orthodox religious terminology on the poem. A more positive explanation of the use of *major* might be the general insistence throughout the poem that Macao is a place of only minor "childish vices," a place where sins of grown-up dimensions are out of place. In any case, Auden now speaks of "mortal sins." Where before he had spoken of "the heart" being killed by these sins, he now speaks of "the strong." "The heart" is universal—all hearts, anyone's heart, hearts in general. But the revised line that singles out "the strong" as victims of "mortal sins" emphasizes the fact that this is a town of small people, low, weak, full of "childish vices" and "the low virtues of the child," people who are the antithesis of the strong, who accomplish on a great scale but, in their greatness, commit the greatest sins. In this town (not even a city), mortal sins need not be feared, for they are the nemesis of the strong, those worthy of being tested by great temptations. This change clearly enhances the effect of the entire portrait, further emphasizing the absence in Macao of high seriousness and a sense of responsibility. One might even say that Macao, suffering from arrested growth of the spirit, has never matured sufficiently to discover moral reality, a failure that Auden makes explicit in the final stanza.

The last line of this tercet, presenting further havoc wrought by "the major sins," stands in the original version as "And governments and men are torn to pieces." This has been recast as "And limbs and governments are torn to pieces," startling us by the abrupt juxtaposition of the graphic piece of human anatomy with the abstract, relatively unevocative political concept. The syllepsis, if such it can be called, is definitely more effective now that "men" has been replaced by the synecdoche "limbs," proving that the part can sometimes be more than the whole.

The revisions of this poem combine to reinforce the basic impression suggested by the original portrayal, that of Macao as a frivolous town which the Catholic Church, winking at its misbehavior, nourishes and protects like an infant sprawling in innocent selfishness.

Although in *Journey to a War* "Macao" and "Hongkong" conclude the section entitled "London to Hongkong," in *CSP*, the group, now retitled "A Voyage," concludes with "A Major Port," formerly sonnet XXV in the sonnet sequence "In Time of War." This sonnet, in spite of having been transferred from one group of poems to another and given its own fresh title, remains largely unaltered.

from "In Time of War" (*Journey to a War*)
XXV

Nothing is given: we must find our law.
Great buildings jostle in the sun for domination;
Behind them stretch like sorry vegetation
The low recessive houses of the poor.

We have no destiny assigned us:
Nothing is certain but the body; we plan
To better ourselves; the hospitals alone remind us
Of the equality of man.

Children are really loved here, even by police:
They speak of years before the big were lonely,
And will be lost.
                          And only
The brass bands throbbing in the parks foretell
Some future reign of happiness and peace.

We learn to pity and rebel. (Auden, *Journey* 14)

A Major Port (*CSP*)

No guidance can be found in ancient lore:
Banks jostle in the sun for domination,
Behind them stretch like sorry vegetation
The low recessive houses of the poor.

We have no destiny assigned us,
No data but our bodies: we plan
To better ourselves; bleak hospitals alone remind us
Of the equality of man.

Children are really loved here, even by police:
They speak of years before the big were lonely.
Here will be no recurrence.

                Only
The brass-bands throbbing in the parks foretell
Some future reign of happiness and peace.

We learn to pity and rebel. (Auden, *CSP* 121–22)

"A Major Port" has a rhyme scheme of ABBA CDC EFF GEG. As already noted, the atypical rhyme pattern of its quatrains matches that of "Hong Kong." It is a modified Petrarchan sonnet, with its tercets linked by a displacement of the ending of one to a position just above the start of the other. Six of the rhyming pairs form perfect rhymes, three masculine and three feminine. The remaining pair form a consonance.

"A Major Port" continues the depiction of the West's invasion of the East. Quickly establishing the ironic disparity between the banks of the financiers and the "low recessive houses of the poor," it goes on to say, "bleak hospitals alone remind us / Of the equality of man." The poem concludes with a humanistic line of defiance, set off from the two preceding lines with which it normally would form a tercet: "We learn to pity and rebel."

The first line of the poem is changed from "Nothing is given: we must find our law" to "No guidance can be found in ancient lore." This revision emphasizes the sudden unaccountable incursion of the modern western world into the technologically backward, ancient East. The banks jostling like Darwinian monsters "in the sun for domination" are something new, something that the East has never had to cope with before. It cannot help itself, nor can it help the western invaders. Neither its ancient lore nor their modern know-how can help the outsiders find their destiny. The revision also serves to make the line's consonance rhyme for poor more respectable by introducing "lore" with its true *r*. Auden mentions this kind of revision in his foreword to *CSP*, saying, "It makes me wince when I see how ready I was to treat -*or* and -*aw* as homophones. It is true that in the Oxonian dialect I speak they are, but that isn't really an adequate excuse" (Auden, *CSP* 16).

In "Hong Kong" Auden states: "Here in the East our bankers have erected / A worthy temple to the Comic Muse." The change in the second line of "A Major Port" ties it closely to the earlier poem, for the relatively vague "Great buildings" become "Banks," the edifices of the already identified invaders, struggling like giants for domination, while the true East remains quietly suffering in the background, manifested in "The low recessive houses of the poor" which "stretch like sorry vegetation" behind the great banks. While revision makes the nature of the interloper clearer (he is concerned primarily with secular success, with money), the syllabic count of the line is reduced from thirteen syllables to eleven, the standard count for a line of iambic pentameter ending in a feminine rhyme.

In the second stanza "Nothing is certain but the body" becomes "No data but our bodies." The effect of the revision is to accentuate the cold, hard, mathematical reality we create for ourselves in our technological western world. The rather ordinary rhetorical pattern of "Nothing is certain" is replaced by the staccato effect of "No data but . . . " in which each syllable is sharp and short and punctuated by an explosive *d* or *t* or, at its weakest, *b*. The word *data* in itself, beyond the effect of its sound, carries with it connotations of dryness and mechanical dehumanization. This marks the second time that Auden has eliminated the word "certain" in search of a stronger effect, "As certain as" giving way to "Convincing as" in "Whither?"

The half-line ending the third stanza has been changed from "And will be lost" to "Here will be no recurrence." I assume that this sentence refers back to the preceding line, "They speak of years before the big were lonely," and suggests that the good times of the past will not return for the big ones, the bankers. The original line suffers from a vagueness, no clear-cut subject for the predicate offering itself, though "they," the speakers, seem the most likely candidate. In any case, the revision brings the syllabic count for the interrupted line from an atypical seven up to the standard ten.

There are a few minor punctuation changes in this poem, two definite articles are replaced by other modifiers ("the body" becomes "our bodies" and "the hospitals" becomes "bleak hospitals"), and two conjunctions are omitted, one in each of the half lines that mark the end of the first tercet and the beginning of the second. I have already noted this tendency to reduce the number of definite articles and conjunctions. We will see more evidence of it in the "Sonnets from China."

In these six poems we have a fair sampling of the technical concerns that Auden reveals in his revising. We see his massive assault on the arrogant and didactic definite article; a lesser, though still notable assault on the facilely mythologizing connective *and*; and a persistent attempt to introduce active verb and verbals, and precise, specific modifiers, verbs and nouns, in place of generalizations and static, looming abstractions.

Chapter Three

Sonnets from China

In *Journey to a War*, "London to Hongkong" was followed by Isherwood's two hundred and twenty-six page "Travel-Diary" and Auden's thirty-two-page collection of photographs called "Picture Commentary." Then came "In Time of War," subtitled "Sonnet Sequence with a verse commentary." In *CSP*, the entire verse commentary is dropped. The sonnet sequence, retitled "Sonnets from China," has dropped six of its original twenty-seven sonnets. A seventh, number XXV, has become "A Major Port," while *Journey to a War*'s dedicatory poem, "To E.M. Forster," now concludes the sonnet sequence.

Remarking on this group of poems in his study *A Reader's Guide to W.H. Auden*, John Fuller says that "In its discussion of evil, of human nature and society, 'Sonnets from China' is Auden's *Essay on Man*" (Fuller 125). Certainly it is a wide-ranging examination of man, presenting concise studies of peasant-farmer, soldier-explorer, scientist, and poet, while tracing the historical progress of Western civilization from a philosophical and ethical perspective. Beginning with a somewhat Darwinized presentation of Genesis, Auden recapitulates the history of fallen man's efforts and sufferings in a world of painfully intermingled freedom and necessity. Scenes of Europe's past and its failures are followed by scenes from the Sino-Japanese War in which the human condition is seen to consist of man suffering evil at the hands of other men. Rarely optimistic, these poems, examining the human being in stark moral terms, seek to formulate a morally and psychologically true picture of that ambivalent creature. Though in a poem of particular hopefulness, Auden, speaking of those who have lived natural, good and selfless lives, guardedly suggests, "If we allow them, they can breathe again: / Happy their wish and mild to flower and flood," the lines which really summarize the entire work in a poetic crystallization of the human condition are: "We live in freedom by necessity, / A mountain people dwelling among mountains" (Auden, *CSP* 136).

The same types of revisions that characterize the poems composing "A Voyage" appear throughout this sonnet sequence. Fastidious elimination of definite articles, constant attention to specificity and detail, revisions of verbs, nouns, adjectives, and whole locutions, a general sharpening of expression and increased variety of phraseology, and a pervasive tinkering with punctuation all play a large part in the revisions these poems have undergone.

The poems in this sonnet sequence are cast without exception in the basic Petrarchan structure of two quatrains followed by two tercets. Auden enjoys varying his rhyming combinations much as does Rilke, whose influence on the original sequence is unmistakable, and, although the twenty-one sonnets retained in *CSP* all have the same stanzaic structure, he manages to use sixteen different rhyme schemes.

The octaves conservatively follow the traditional patterns of ABAB CDCD and ABBA CDDC, with the exception, already noted, of sonnet XXI, "To E.M. Forster," which, in its revised form, displays the mixed pattern ABBA CDCD. However in the tercets, Auden juggles his patterns most ingeniously, utilizing almost all possible rhyming combinations. We will see these diverse variations as we examine the individual sonnets.

I *(Journey to a War)*

So from the years the gifts were showered; each
Ran off with his at once into his life:
Bee took the politics that make a hive,
Fish swam as fish, peach settled into peach.

And were successful at the first endeavor;
The hour of birth their only time at college
They were content with their precocious knowledge,
And knew their station and were good for ever.

Till finally there came a childish creature
On whom the years could model any feature,
And fake with ease a leopard or a dove;

Who by the lightest wind was changed and shaken,
And looked for truth and was continually mistaken,
And envied his few friends and chose his love. (Auden,
Journey 247)

I *(Collected Shorter Poems)*

So from the years their gifts were showered: each
Grabbed at the one it needed to survivor;
Bee took the politics that suit a hive,
Trout finned as trout, peach moulded into peach,

> And were successful at their first endeavor.
> The hour of birth their only time in college,
> They were content with their precocious knowledge,
> To know their station and be right for ever.
>
> Till, finally, there came a childish creature
> On whom the years could model any feature,
> Fake, as chance fell, a leopard or a dove,
>
> Who by the gentlest wind was rudely shaken,
> Who looked for truth but always was mistaken,
> And envied his few friends, and chose his love. (Auden, *CSP* 128)

Sonnet I has a rhyme scheme of ABBA CDDC EEF GGF. Eight lines end in feminine rhymes. Though this proportion of feminine endings is higher than the average for these sonnets, it is not a startling departure by any means. Sonnets four and five, for example, have ten feminine endings each. It is clear that Auden does not shy away from employing feminine endings, managing them with such success that they serve equally well in light and serious verses. The lines are iambic pentameter, the preferred meter in this sonnet sequence. Each line with a feminine ending is allowed an eleventh syllable. This seems to be Auden's general practice throughout the sequence though certain exceptions will be noted.

Sonnet I deals with the Creation. It speaks of insect, fish, and fruit and how they immediately become themselves, "successful at their first endeavor." They are the subject of the octet and are contrasted with man, the subject of the sestet, for they "know their station and [are] right for ever," whereas man is described as "a childish creature . . . / Who looked for truth but always was mistaken, / And envied his friends and chose his love." The painful privilege of the human condition, involving freedom, quest, failure, and dissatisfaction, stands clear against the foil of the simple success and limited contentedness of all other forms of life.

Almost all of the fairly extensive revisions in this poem serve to localize, particularize, and clarify through detail. Though most of the changes involve a movement from the general to the specific, some are calculated to correct false suggestions or implications of already specific but ill-chosen words. That Auden's methodical search for *le mot juste* is generally successful (he cherished *two* sets of the unabridged Oxford English Dictionary) should become clear as this study progresses.

In the very first line we encounter a fairly inconspicuous example of Auden's standard treatment of his definite article. Here, as in the first line of the second stanza, *the* becomes *their*. The effect is to emphasize the actual creatures and fruits of the creation. The abstract, archetypal sounding "the gifts" becomes specifically "their gifts," now clearly assigned, and "the first endeavor." Such changes are endemic in the revised sonnet sequence, and this poem is remarkable for the fact that its revised form eliminates only two definite articles.

Strict with his former favorite, the conjunction *and*, Auden drops this typically Germanic device four times, rejecting it, I would imagine, as a too facile means of creating a mythic mood while producing smooth lines and easy transitions. Three of the conjunctions which have been dropped were in the initial position in lines eight, eleven, and thirteen. Throughout his revisions, as we shall see, Auden has striven with particular care to reduce the vast number of lines beginning with *and*. His earlier practice in this respect resulted in sonnets with up to ten lines commencing with the omnipresent conjunction, but in *CSP* only one sonnet has as many as four initial *and*'s, while most seem to have a respectable two.

The second line of sonnet I is radically revised: "Ran off with his at once into his life" becomes "Grabbed at the one it needed to survive." The new verbs and the added infinitive convert a rather relaxed prose-like narration into a line with sharpness and a kind of threatening vitality.

Grab, descended from Middle Low German, has a slangy contemporary ring to it implying haste and greed. It is a violent verb, particularly in conjunction with the preposition *at*, which emphasizes the ugly suddenness of the instinctive act. "Grabbed at," with its generally lower-class associations, replaces "ran off with," an antiseptic middle-class expression devoid of any visceral or visual force. It seems to me that the effectiveness of the new verb is much enhanced by the abrupt initial stress of the trochaic inversion it brings to the line. In the expression "ran off with," the stress falls easily enough on the second word, fitting comfortably into the regular iambic pattern, thereby doing nothing to enliven metrically an unexciting formulation. The other new verb in the line, "need," has become popular through the agency of those thriving modern disciplines, psychology and psychiatry, and further intensifies the feeling of pressure and desperation involved in the struggle for survival.

Need is a word that brooks no contradiction and allows for no appeal. In its primal finality, coupled with the unambiguous infinitive "to survive" it effectively complements the initial verb to give a sense both of great urgency and blind instinct. Not only is this line less tame and more evocative, it also provides a perfect rhyme with line three ("survive-hive"), in place of a near rhyme ("life-hive").

A small but interesting revision appears in line three. Instead of "Bee took the politics that make a hive," we have "Bee took the politics that suit a hive." This change in the verb seems justifiable on two accounts. The revision is more accurate, for, though the politics of the bees are a part of the hive and essential to it in its present form, they alone do not "make" it. They do "suit" it. More important is the change in tone that the revision effects. The primal, basic, all-encompassing, but common and unevocative verb "make" is replaced by the cosmopolitan, refined term "suit," which is much more appropriate to the metaphor drawn from sophisticated man, "politics."

Line four is significantly revised: "Fish swam as fish, peach settled into peach" becomes "Trout finned as trout, peach moulded into peach." Noun and verb are both changed from the general to the specific. Statement becomes image as "fish," the generic term of a whole class, is replaced by "trout," the name of a particular kind of fish with a particular, individual, identifiable look. At the same time, the ordinary, unevocative verb "swam" is replaced by a verb built from a specific noun, so that "finned," echoing Pope's "finny tribe," speaks not only of silent motion through water but also of something specifically piscatorial, the vibrating or undulating motion of actual fins on a living trout. John Whitehead, in a review of *CSP*, singles out this change as an example of the desire to extinguish "excessive sibilants" (Whitehead, "Vin Audenaire" 492). Though the revision may have been intended to accomplish this end, it seems more likely, from an overall consideration of Auden's revising procedure in these sonnets, that his primary concern here was to move from the general to the specific.

The second image in the line, that of a "peach," is already specific, so it remains unchanged. However the verb undergoes a transformation. "Moulded," emphasizing the idea of creation as a living, shaping process, replaces the more passive "settled," with its quiet intimation of a destiny gently discovered and acquiesced in. The change in verb might reflect a change in perspective from the Darwinian to the teleological view. Whatever its purpose, the revision deprives us of the special felicity of the original, in which the temper of the verb suited so well the delicacy of the fruit around it.

In the second stanza, besides the elimination of the definite article, already noted, and a minor punctuation change, there is a major transformation in the final line. Speaking of non-human forms of life, Auden says, in the earlier version: "They were content with their precocious knowledge, / And knew their station and were good for ever." The last line has been revised to read: "To know their station and be right for ever," a change that alters the meaning of the line. In place of the Rilkean mythologizing "and," which gives a false effect of more and more information being piled up, the infinitive, neatly in apposition with the previous line, leads to a succinct and limiting elaboration of it. Line seven, as we now see, could well have ended with a colon. The elimination of the conjunction and the insertion of the infinitive implies that "their precocious knowledge" is simply the knowledge of their place in life, "their station." That is apparently all they know, but it is enough, for it makes them "right," though not "good." *Right* has significantly different overtones from *good*. In the moral realm the latter is the ultimate, implying spiritual excellence and virtue. It is a quality and a goal reserved for choosing creatures who, conscious and self-conscious, make free choices. Without consciousness and without conscience, the concepts of good and evil become meaningless. *Right* is also an ultimate of sorts, but in the secular world of specific problems and limited questions. It carries with it the connotations of correct, proper, fitting, appropriate, and that is just what the non-human creations are by their very nature. Without freedom of will they immediately and instinctively find their niche in life and remain there forever, *right*, but not *good*. The meaning clearly has been altered, and I think the alteration is for the best. The change reflects a precision and care in dealing with distinctions in moral philosophy that apparently was lacking at the time of the earlier version.

The only important change in the third stanza is puzzling. Referring to man, Auden says: " . . . a childish creature / On whom the years could model any feature, / And fake with ease a leopard or a dove." The last line becomes: "Fake, as chance fell, a leopard or a dove." Though acknowledging the euphonious alliterative effect of *f*'s and *l*'s achieved by the revision, I am surprised at the apparent implication that chance determines what a man becomes. This seems to contradict the idea of man's unique burden of freedom, an idea that lies implicit behind the entire sonnet sequence. Either the line is surprisingly out of character or, more probably, I have failed to understand it.

There are a number of interesting changes in the last stanza. The first line, "Who by the lightest wind was changed and shaken," becomes in the revised poem "Who by the gentlest wind was rudely shaken." The softness of "gentlest" is balanced against the new adverb, "rudely," emphasizing the bewildered weakness of the "childish creature." Perhaps the perfectly balanced antithesis of noun and modifier against verb and modifier is a bit too pat. In any case, "rudely shaken" makes "changed" quite unnecessary since it sufficiently, even graphically, suggests the fickleness and instability of the human creature.

The penultimate line of the poem has been changed from "And looked for truth and was continually mistaken" to "Who looked for truth but always was mistaken." Not only are the two completely superfluous conjunctions eliminated, but the rhythm is clearly improved, conforming now to the general iambic flow that prevails throughout the sonnet. In the earlier version "continually" with its four or five syllables disrupts the flow of the line and forces its syllabic count beyond conventional bounds. In a poem where no other line has more than the eleven syllables allowed to iambic pentameter lines ending with a feminine rhyme, this line, unrevised, has fourteen or, if one charitably slurs over the adjacent vowels, thirteen syllables. Quite simply, the revised line manages to convey the same message, conform to the demands of the iambic pentameter pattern, yet retain the tone of the natural speaking voice.

In summary, a conversion of general and abstract to specific and precise is quite evident in this poem and manifests itself in the revision of verbs, nouns, adjectives, and adverbs. The elimination of repetitive, incantatory conjunctions is more apparent here than a similar tendency, noted throughout "A Voyage," to reduce the number of definite articles. Noteworthy, because rarely needed, is the revision that brings the metrical count of the penultimate line into conformity with the conventional pattern.

II (*Journey to a War*)

> They wondered why the fruit had been forbidden;
> It taught them nothing new. They hid their pride,
> But did not listen much when they were chidden;
> They knew exactly what to do outside.
>
> They left: immediately the memory faded
> Of all they'd learnt; they could not understand
> The dogs now who, before, had always aided;
> The stream was dumb with whom they'd always planned.
>
> They wept and quarreled: freedom was so wild.
> In front, maturity, as he ascended,
> Retired like a horizon from the child;
>
> The dangers and the punishments grew greater;
> And the way back by angels was defended
> Against the poet and the legislator. (Auden, *Journey* 247–48)

II (*Collected Shorter Poems*)

> They wondered why the fruit had been forbidden:
> It taught them nothing new. They hid their pride,
> But did not listen when they were chidden:
> They knew exactly what to do outside.
>
> They left. Immediately the memory faded
> Of all they'd known: they could not understand
> The dogs now who before had always aided;
> The stream was dumb with whom they'd always planned.

> They wept and quarreled: freedom was so wild.
> In front maturity as he ascended
> Retired like a horizon from the child,
> The dangers and the punishments grew greater,
> And the way back by angels was defended
> Against the poet and the legislator. (Auden, *CSP* 128)

Sonnet II follows a rhyming pattern of ABAB CDCD EFE GFG. This pattern appears again in sonnets VIII and XVIII. Again, as in sonnet I there are eight feminine endings, each affixing to its line an eleventh syllable. The other lines are regularly decasyllabic.

The poem continues the retelling of the story of Genesis. Man has already eaten the forbidden fruit, has learned nothing from it, leaves the garden, finds himself alone and unaided for the first time, cries, argues with his mate, is confronted by wild freedom, and finds it hard to mature. Though life becomes harder and harder, he cannot turn back, for angels defend the lost garden.

Only one word has been changed in this poem, but there are ten revisions involving punctuation. Although, in general, I find Auden's punctuation changes relatively inconsequential, these demand examination. Throughout the sonnet sequence I have made it my practice to note all punctuation changes but mention only those that seem to me of some significance. In this poem there are three lines in the octet which end, in the earlier version, in semicolons. The first two of these semicolons have been converted to colons as has a semi-colon appearing in the middle of the sixth line of the poem. The effect of these changes is to give tighter unity to connected ideas, particularly in the first stanza where the cause and effect relationship within each of the two pairs of statements is accentuated by the colon. Two sets of optional parenthetical commas have been dropped, those in line seven surrounding "before," and those in line ten surrounding "maturity." In lines eleven and twelve terminal semicolons become commas, a sensible replacement. It is worth noting that Auden has dropped five out of the six semicolons he originally employed in this poem. I consider this reduction in the number of semicolons, an exercise adhered to throughout the sonnet sequence, most beneficial, for the semicolon has become a rather indeterminate punctuation sign, allowing too much leeway to both lazy poet and lazy reader. The only other punctuation change occurs in line five where the colon is replaced by a period, making even more final and irreversible our progenitors' departure from the garden of Eden: "They left. Immediately the memory faded."

Even a cursory examination of "Sonnets from China" suggests that Auden's revisions of punctuation are more likely a case of uneasy tinkering than a systematic effort for uniformity of usage. A comparison of these poems as they appear in *CSP* with the English text on facing pages of the

Italian *Opere Poetiche, di W.H. Auden,* published in February 1966, reveals, in fact, much inconsistency in Auden's practice. In the short period between the publication of the two books, Auden made only a few revisions involving language (several of these are of great interest and will be discussed later); however, he made extensive changes in punctuation. Sonnet II provides a typical example of these late alterations. Here are the second and third stanzas as they appear in *Opere Poetiche:*

> They left: immediately the memory faded
> Of all they'd known; they could not understand
> The dogs now, who before had always aided,
> The stream was dumb with whom they'd always planned.
> They wept and quarreled; freedom was so wild.
> In front, maturity as he ascended
> Retired like a horizon from the child. (Auden, *Opere Poetiche)*

In the first line above, the colon of the original is retained, whereas the version in *CSP* converts it to a period, strengthening the impression of suddenness and finality in their departure. Though in the second line above the solitary word change in the poem has already occurred, "learnt" becoming "known," the conversion of the semicolon has not. This particular revision, however, seems of questionable value, in any case. In the original, the third line has unnecessary commas surrounding "before" and an appropriate semicolon at the end. Though the unnecessary commas are dropped in both revised versions, only the version in *Opere Poetiche* adds a sensible comma after "now." On the other hand it also, rather gratuitously, replaces the original's inoffensive and appropriate semicolon with an unfortunate comma. The version in *CSP* returns to the more useful semicolon of the original. In the first line of the tercet, *Opere Poetiche* introduces a semi-colon after "quarreled," but *CSP* returns to the original colon. In the second line, of the original's three commas, *Opere Poetiche* retains only the first, while *CSP* discards all three. It seems to me that the original version is the most readily intelligible.

Opere Poetiche's mixture of old practice retained, new practice established and repeated in *CSP*, new practice carried even further in *CSP*, and, most bewilderingly, new practice abandoned for a return to the original in *CSP* suggests that Auden is uncertain of his preferences in punctuation. Since the late punctuation changes in Sonnet II, revealed by a comparison of the texts in *Opere Poetiche* and *CSP*, are representative of those in the rest of the sequence, I will not discuss such discrepancies in future poems.

The only word change in this poem, as already noted, occurs in the second line of the second stanza, when we are told that upon leaving Eden our progenitors forgot "all they'd learnt." This becomes "all they'd known," a revision of some importance, as it involves a theological correction. They had not really learned anything in the garden, for it had all been given to them; they had *known* without learning. Learning, involving trial and error, pain and pleasure, begins only after the fall.

III (*Journey to a War*)

Only a smell had feelings to make known,
Only an eye could point in a direction;
The fountain's utterance was itself alone;
The bird meant nothing: that was his projection

Who named it as he hunted it for food.
He felt the interest in his throat, and found
That he could send his servant to the wood,
Or kiss his bride to rapture with a sound.

They bred like locusts till they hid the green
And edges of the world: and he was abject,
And to his own creation became subject;

And shook with hate for things he'd never seen,
And knew of love without love's proper object,
And was oppressed as he had never been. (Auden, *Journey* 248)

III (*CSP*)

Only a smell had feelings to make known,
Only an eye could point in a direction,
The fountain's utterance was itself alone:
He, though, by naming thought to make connection

Between himself as hunter and his food;
He felt the interest in his throat and found
That he could send a servant to chop wood
Or kiss a girl to rapture with a sound.

They bred like locusts till they hid the green
And edges of the world: confused and abject,
A creature to his own creation subject,

He shook with hate for things he'd never seen,
Pined for a love abstracted from its object,
And was oppressed as he had never been. (Auden, *CSP* 129)

Sonnet III has a rhyme pattern of ABAB CDCD EFF EFE. Five lines end in feminine rhymes and accordingly have an eleventh syllable. All other lines are decasyllabic. Though the metrics of this poem are highly regular, we encounter, for the first time in the revised sonnet sequence, imperfect rhymes. In this poem Auden introduces a sight-rhyme, "food-wood," and a consonance, "abject-subject-object." Other deviations from the perfect rhyme will be remarked upon as they are met in the remaining poems of the sequence.

Sonnet III deals with man's growth and development in the world, his discovery of his senses and his desires as well as some of his powers, and his confused slavery, through love and hate, to his own creation—the abstract idea.

Four lines are significantly revised, affecting the meaning, the meter, and the clarity of the poem. Lines four and five have been thoroughly recast:

> The bird meant nothing: that was his projection
> Who named it as he hunted it for food.

Becomes:

> He, though, by naming thought to make connection
> Between himself as hunter and his food;

The revision accomplishes several ends. It clearly focuses attention upon man and his actions and attitudes from the very first. It concentrates upon man's attempt to relate everything to himself for his own use by naming it, thus placing and freezing it, denying it any purpose of its own, any sense of its existence independent of his need. Man's valiant effort is made somehow pitiable, however, by the untamed, untainted voice of flowing water: "The fountain's utterance was itself alone." Man, not content merely to exist, must name so as to order and control. When he names an animal, he names his prey. Of course, he must still catch and kill the animal, but naming it is a first step to domination. The earlier version pictures man dismissing the significance of the creature's life while naming it, "The bird meant nothing: that was his projection, / Who named it as he hunted it for food," but it does not really go into the subject of man's use of speech as a means to order and control the world around him. The revised version, however, takes the hint of a suggestion from the earlier version and, developing it, adds to the growing man a new dimension, a dimension of particular interest to a poet, a worker in words.

Line eleven is recast from "And to his own creation became subject" to "A creature to his own creation subject." This marks a vast improvement in the rhythm of the verse, for in the unrevised line the progression of regular iambic feet is roughly interrupted and disjointed by the awkward anapestic intrusion caused by "became." The metrical flow of the line is improved and the meaning has deepened, for now we are reminded that the man who is becoming subject to what he has created, namely ideas, is himself a created thing, "a creature."

The penultimate line of the poem has been significantly changed: "And knew of love without love's proper object." Not only has the repetitious initial conjunction been eliminated, as it has in the two lines that precede this one, but a new verb with emotional associations is introduced, though for ironic purposes, replacing the unevocative "knew." At the same time the meaning seems to have been expanded. In its earlier form, the line simply states that man possesses an emotion without having found the "proper object" for it. This provides a kind of variation in counterpoint to the previous line, elaborating upon its implied message: "And shook with hate for things he'd never seen." We are shown the human creature who, having discovered his strength, particularly that implicit in the power of speech, the power of naming things, now discovers ideas and quickly becomes so entangled in them that his emotions of love and hate wander lost among them, free of any tangible object to draw and control them. It is this aspect of man's complex development that John Fuller addresses when he speaks of the danger of language, "Which, though it gives man power, exercises its own tyranny . . . by obsessing man with ideas removed from reality" (Fuller, *Reader's Guide* 126). The revised line seems to add to this picture the suggestion that man is not merely capable of abstractions and of attaching his emotions to abstractions, but he prefers dealing in the vast and nebulous rather than confronting objective reality's limited incarnations. I read the line as fruitfully ambiguous. Does man yearn consciously and specifically for a love "abstracted from its object," or is it merely a fact that he pines for a love which, without his awareness, is abstracted from its object?

A number of lesser revisions deserve mention. Only two definite articles are dropped, one in line four ("The bird meant nothing . . . "), and one in line seven as noted below. More important, three of the five conjunctive "and's" that begin the last five lines of the poem are replaced, resulting in a beneficial variety of phraseology. In line seven, Auden has changed "That he could send his servant to the wood" to "That he could send a servant to the wood." A verbal replaces a prepositional phrase, and discernable activity enters the line. The new tableau provides not only a specific visual image but also an illustrative manifestation of the service demanded by master of man. The added detail of chopping wood functions both logically and visually to give the image greater effect. A distinctiveness and focus is gained which the earlier version, speaking only of a servant sent to the wood, lacks. In the eighth line "kiss his bride" becomes "kiss a girl," a generous formulation eschewing prudery. Economy is served in line ten as "and he was abject" becomes "confused and abject," the subject of those modifiers being introduced conveniently and efficiently two lines later.

In this sonnet, revision has resulted in a greater clarity and extension of ideas, increased economy, improved metrics, and expanded imagery. As in most of the revised sonnets, though here to a lesser extent than usual, definite articles and conjunctive and's are eliminated while verbs and verbals are added. The replacement of semicolons, Auden's early favorites, with colons and commas, a habitual revision already remarked upon in sonnet II, continues.

IV (*Journey to a War*)

He stayed: and was imprisoned in possession.
The seasons stood like guards about his ways,
The mountains chose the mother of his children,
And like a conscience the sun ruled his days.

Beyond him his young cousins in the city
Pursued their rapid and unnatural course,
Believed in nothing but were easy-going,
And treated strangers like a favourite horse.

And he changed little,
But took his colour from the earth,
And grew in likeness to his sheep and cattle.

The townsman thought him miserly and simple,
The poet wept and saw in him the truth,
And the oppressor held him up as an example. (Auden, *Journey* 248–49)

IV (*CSP*)

He stayed, and was imprisoned in possession:
By turns the seasons guarded his one way,
The mountains chose the mother of his children,
In lieu of conscience the sun ruled his day.

Beyond him, his young cousins in the city
Pursued their rapid and unnatural courses,
Believed in nothing but were easy-going,
Far less afraid of strangers than of horses.

He, though, changed little,
But took his colour from the earth,
And grew in likeness to his fowls and cattle.

The townsman thought him miserly and simple,
Unhappy poets took him for the truth,
And tyrants held him up as an example. (Auden, *CSP* 129)

Sonnet IV has a rhyme scheme of ABAB CDCD FGF HGH. The octave
displays a regular alteration of distant slant rhyme with full rhyme. In both
quatrains lines two and four end in full rhymes, while lines one and three contribute the weak slant rhymes of unaccented syllables. In the first quatrain the
slant rhyme is provided by the unaccented terminal syllables of the end words
"possession-children." In the second quatrain the slant rhyme of "city" with
"easy-going" also depends upon unaccented final syllables, but the rhyme is
somewhat hidden by the fact that it appears, in line four, buried in the middle
of the hyphenated final word.

The pattern in the tercets forms a complex weave of analyzed rhyme. The
accented vowel sounds of the end words of the first lines of each stanza
are identical as are the accented vowel sounds of the end words of the third
lines: "little-simple," "cattle-example." Within each stanza the consonants
following the accented vowels of the end words of lines one and three are
identical: "little-cattle," "simple-example." The consonance of the end words
in the second line of each stanza involves a quietly effective shuffle of the
r sound: "earth-truth." As Babette Deutsch says while discussing the complexities of Auden's analyzed rhyme in her *Poetry Handbook*: "Such a *tour
de force* is of course unusual" (Deutsch, *Poetry Handbook* 127).

There are ten lines with feminine endings and four with masculine, one of
each deviating from the established syllabic count. Line nine, instead of the
expected eleven syllables, has but five, while line ten, instead of the expected
ten, has but eight. The two atypical lines, occurring as they do at the start of
the first tercet, give an added weight to the traditional break between octave
and sestet, while moving evenly, in gentle syllabic increments of three, back
to the norm of eleven in the last line of the stanza.

This poem introduces the divergent development of evolving man. It
concentrates upon the earthbound peasant, the rural worker tied to nature,
and contrasts him with "his young cousins in the city" who, progressing far
beyond him in the pursuit of their "unnatural courses, / Believed in nothing." In the octave, stanza one shows nature's hold upon the peasant, while
stanza two presents the dubious superiority of the city dweller. In the sestet,
the first tercet further identifies the peasant with the earth and its creatures,
who are now his creatures as well. The second tercet presents three attitudes

toward the benighted natural man: the condescension of civilized townsmen, the romantic admiration of unhappy poets, and the exploitative indifference of hypocritical tyrants. In this sonnet three lines are largely revised and four partially. The second line in the opening quatrain, "The seasons stood like guards about his ways," is recast as "By turns the seasons guarded his one way." Though all men are bound to some degree by necessity, the peasant is, by his utter dependence upon nature, more visibly bound than most. The seasons dictating when he must plow, sow, tend, reap, and lie low, his whole life is determined by natural processes as the "unnatural courses" of his city cousins are not. Yet within the strictures of his bonds, even he is free to labor diligently or poorly. The revision of this line intensifies the sense of the peasant's bondage to nature and of the necessity intrinsic to his condition. Revised or unrevised, the line reminds one of the angels defending the way back to the Garden of Eden in sonnet II, repeating the motif of fallen man's obligatory "freedom" in a world of necessity. It is worth noting the replacement of a simile by an implied metaphor in this revision. There will be two more changes involving the elimination of a simile in this sonnet.

An apparently minor change in the last line of the opening quatrain results in a subtle but significant shift in nuance. "And like a conscience the sun ruled his days" becomes "In lieu of conscience the sun ruled his day." The simile is imperfect, for the sun rules quite differently from a conscience, existing as it does outside the world of moral judgements. In fact the whole purpose of introducing the sun is to show that necessity has become the ruling force, displacing the painful blessing of conscience. The replacement of the simile by "in lieu of" draws one to the conclusion that I think Auden wishes to suggest with the earlier line, that the sun is, in fact, a usurper. In revising the line, Auden has dropped a facile simile and an initial "and" while clarifying the verse's intent.

The last line of the second quatrain has been completely turned around. "And treated strangers like a favourite horse" now reads "Far less afraid of strangers than of horses." Again an initial "and" is eliminated, and with it a simile. Though this type of omission may be only incidental to Auden's greater concern of focusing with care some of his less precise lines, still it is worth remarking that the revised poem has lost all three of its similes, two of the losses involving a shift in meaning from a falsely facile equation utilizing "like" to a new and accurate formulation. In the present case the verse is completely reconstructed, the result being a much more sensible statement. Those "young cousins in the city" are most unlikely to have a favorite horse, but, quite to the contrary, are liable to be afraid of horses. Now the line shows the sophisticated city cousins at ease with strangers by presenting this relationship against the foil of their fear of horses. This reversal in the role of horses satisfies the demands of logic and reinforces the image of the city cousins pursuing "their rapid and unnatural courses." The horse, a creature of nature whom man has domesticated, provides a link between man and nature, so it is most appropriate for the city cousins, following their "unnatural courses," to fear them.

The first line of the sestet is revised from "And he changed little" to "He, though, changed little." Not only is another repetitive initial "and" eliminated, but it is replaced by a conjunction which serves its purpose properly, indicating that the connection with the preceding stanza involves a contrast with the city cousin who, in fact, has changed.

In the eleventh line of the poem we are told that the peasant, who "changed little," in fact "grew in likeness to his sheep and cattle." In revising, Auden has replaced sheep with fowls. The image of men becoming like sheep is rather too familiar and tritely symbolic. The peasant's condition of powerless acquiescence is sufficiently suggested by the combination of the less stereotypic "fowls" with "cattle." The shift from "sheep" to "fowls," freeing the verse from an obtrusive dead simile, allows it to convey not only the uncomplaining suffering of these country primitives, but their genuine closeness to nature and its creatures as well.

The penultimate line of the poem has been significantly recast. "The poet wept and saw in him the truth," now reads "Unhappy poets took him for the truth." The revision accomplishes several ends. We can no longer think that this man of the soil is really the truth just because poets may see him as such. "Took him for the truth" tells us what the poets thought while implying their mistake. In conjunction with the added modifier "Unhappy," the new formulation suggests that the poets accepted the peasant as a symbol of truth because they were unhappy with their own reality to begin with. Like the townsman and the tyrant, the poets did not see the man himself, but their idea of him. In the process of revision, Auden has rid the line of an "and" as well as a definite article.

In the last line of the poem, "the oppressor" is changed to "tyrants." This revision involves the elimination of another definite article, the replacement of a term from the jargon of the left by a word free of partisan political overtones, and the reduction of the line from six feet to five.

Revision of this sonnet has resulted in improved precision of expression, achieved principally through careful replacement of facile similes. Of secondary interest is the fact that two definite articles are cut, three initial conjunctive "and's" in lines four, eight, and nine are dropped, and the metrics of the last line are corrected to conform to conventional standards.

V *(Journey to a War)*

His generous bearing was a new invention:
For life was slow; earth needed to be careless:
With horse and sword he drew the girls' attention;
He was the Rich, the Bountiful, the Fearless.

And to the young he came as a salvation;
They needed him to free them from their mothers,
And grew sharp-witted in the long migration,
And round his camp fires learnt all men are brothers.

But suddenly the earth was full: he was not wanted.
And he became the shabby and demented,
And took to drink to screw his nerves to murder;

Or sat in offices and stole,
And spoke approvingly of Law and Order,
And hated life with all his soul. (Auden, *Journey* 249)

V *(CSP)*

His care-free swagger was a fine invention:
Life was too slow, too regular, too grave.
With horse and sword he drew the girls' attention,
A conquering hero, bountiful and brave,

To whom teen-agers looked for liberation:
At his command they left behind their mothers,
Their wits were sharpened by the long migration,
His camp-fires taught them all the horde were brothers.

Till what he came to do was done: unwanted,
Grown seedy, paunchy, pouchy, disappointed,
He took to drink to screw his nerves to murder,

Or sat in offices and stole,
Boomed at his children about Law and Order,
And hated life with heart and soul. (Auden, *CSP* 130)

Sonnet V has a rhyme pattern of ABAB CDCD EEF GFG. In the original, all line endings were feminine with the exception of the last stanza's "stone-soul," but revision replaces the first quatrain's feminine consonance, "careless-Fearless," with the perfect masculine rhyme "grave-brave." In the second quatrain, "liberation" replaces "salvation" as the rhyme word for "migration," so that now even the initial consonants of the accented syllables match. After revision, all verses of the octave end in full rhymes. In the sestet, four of six lines end in consonance in both the original and revised version. The only effect of revision on the rhymes of the sestet is the change of "wanted-demented" to "unwanted-disappointed."

Revision results in some metrical adjustments as well. In the first stanza the second and fourth lines have had their feminine endings replaced by masculine ones, the second line obediently dropping its eleventh syllable and the fourth line, if one assigns but two syllables to "conquering," following suit. The rhythmic alteration of line two, adding effective reinforcement to the meaning of the line, will be discussed below. Metrics remain unchanged in the second quatrain, each line retaining the prescribed eleven syllables. In the first tercet, however, revision reduces line one from thirteen syllables to the appropriate eleven. In the final stanza no metrical changes occur, lines one and three with their masculine rhyme still confined to a curtailed eight syllables.

Sonnet V speaks of the heroic adventurer, the soldier, explorer or pioneer. The octave deals with his appearance, his grandeur, his symbolic and real value to a young world in need of "A conquering hero, bountiful and brave." The sestet moves on to his unhappy obsolescence later when, all marches made, lands explored, aliens defeated, his primitive skills and virtues now more of a nuisance than a glory, the adventurer, pushed into sedentary and unwilling retirement, "unwanted / Grown seedy, paunchy, pouchy, disappointed . . . hated life with heart and soul." The hero is depicted in his early barbaric glory playing an essential role in the evolution of Western civilization, bringing about change and progress to such effect that, ironically, his own virtues become useless if not dangerous, and he finds himself a superannuated conqueror without purpose, place, or meaning.

Revision is more extensive in this poem than in any other in the sonnet sequence. Only two lines remain unchanged, the first stanza's "With horse and sword he drew the girls' attention" and the last stanza's "Or sat in offices and stole."

In the first quatrain's opening line "generous bearing" suggests stateliness and stature, but the noun is static, and the image, accordingly, is neither dramatic nor vivid. "Care-free swagger" is much more evocative, both noun and modifier conveying a sense of brash young freedom, energy, and motion. The revised line introduces an image whose inherent movement, quite unlike the fixed quality of "generous bearing," contrasts most effectively with the idea appearing in the next line that "life was too slow." As for the other change in the line, "new" giving way to "fine," all inventions are, by definition, new, so Auden removes the redundancy, replacing it with an adjective which, though common enough, further fills our impression of the adventurer, suggesting, as it does, that he himself is quite a fine fellow, both in the eyes of others and in his own.

The revised second line is much improved. Its relationship to the first line is more clearly drawn. In the earlier version, the implied contrast between the hero's "generous bearing" and the fact that "life was slow" is not quite clear, nor is the implied kinship of carelessness and generous bearing. Now the second line presents only one image, and that in a rhythm that is "slow . . . regular . . . grave" and appropriately unexciting, contrasting effectively with the jaunty movement introduced by revision into the first line. The serial adjectives, each accompanied by the regularly repeated adverb, tell us what the swaggerer is breaking away from and, by their rhythmic dullness, suggest the necessity of his revolt. The second half of the original line is dropped, but the idea of "careless" is salvaged and used to good effect in a slightly modi- fied form in the revised first line, appearing as it does in "care-free swagger." It is interesting to note that through revision line two has lost one syllable, yet now takes considerably longer to read, slowed as its pace is by the even pauses of the commas between the descriptive modifiers. Now, as it had not before, the rhythm of the line contributes to its meaning.

In the third line the only alteration is the necessary conversion of the final semicolon to a comma, allowing the grammatical transformation of the fol- lowing line from an independent clause to an appositive phrase. The fourth line itself is, in fact, significantly revised. Auden has rid the line of its capital- ized, substantivized adjectives, stripping them of their accompanying definite articles and returning them to their simple adjectival function. At the same time, "He was" is effectively replaced by the appositive construction "A con- quering hero," which gives a name to what is being described, thereby helping to crystallize the descriptive fragments of the stanza into a complete image. "Rich" seems superfluous next to "bountiful," so it is dropped. "Bountiful," retained, is joined by the alliterating "brave" in place of "Fearless." As noted earlier, the perfect rhyme of "grave-brave" has replaced the consonance of "careless-Fearless" in lines two and four.

Stanza two is entirely revised. In line one, "the young," with its suggestion of energy, eagerness, potential, and future, is replaced by "teen-agers," with its suggestion of facility, haste, shallowness, incompleteness, and irresponsi- bility. "Salvation," with its religious overtones, is replaced by "liberation," a word which, in conjunction with teen-agers, evokes an image of anxious half-formed creatures seeking an outlet for the heat within them and a free- dom in which to stretch and grow. Liberation, it is true, may give them room for anything, but it in no way guarantees salvation, though to the teen-agers themselves liberation and salvation may appear to be synonymous. Whether the hero really will free the teenagers is left in doubt by the revised construc- tion which tells us only that they looked to him for liberation. The revised line leaves itself open to an ironic reading quite in consonance with the unhappy developments depicted in the sestet. The conquering hero's sorry fate is not unanticipated.

This revised line contains three technical changes worth mentioning. The change in verb and final abstract noun results in the alliterative effect of "*l*ooked for *l*iberation." The introduction of "teen-agers" into the line allows the elimination of a definite article. But most noteworthy of all is the fact that an initial "and" is dropped from the line. This is the first of six initial uses of "and" to be cut in this poem. We have already seen three initial connectives eliminated in sonnets I, III, and IV. This former practice of Auden's, already noted, of stringing together line after line of descriptive narrative with the all-purpose, initial "and" appears in many of the earlier versions of these sonnets.

Throughout his revisions, Auden consistently pares down to the barest minimum his use of this initial "and." Often he will cut all but the one at the head of the last line, thereby giving to that line a certain weight and finality that it could not have had if it were merely the last in a longish series of lines linked by the initial "and." Often, as is the case here in stanza two, the repeated connectives are quite expendable. Their presence, rather than performing an essential grammatical function, serves, like that of glowing candles in a dimly lit restaurant, to create an atmosphere of heightened emotion and romance. Their danger to the poet is clear. Relying on their hypnotic effect to mesmerize the reader, he may neglect to give his images the acuity they would need to hold up under a cold, bright light. The triumph of atmosphere may easily foster what it so well can hide—a vagueness of imagery.

This practice, against which Auden has taken up revisionary arms, was undoubtedly nurtured by Rilke, one of his strongest early influences. In sonnet XIX Auden turns for inspiration to the image of Rilke patiently waiting for Muzot for the return of his voice. It was, in fact, in the castle of Muzot that Rilke wrote *Sonnets to Orpheus*, from which the following example of his use of the romanticizing *und* is taken:

> Und fast ein Madchen wars und ging hervor
> aus diesem einiger, Gluck von San und Leter
> und glanzte klar durch ihre Fruhlingsschleier
> und machte sich ein Bott in in meinem Chr.
> Und schlief in mir. Und alles war ihr Schiaf (Rilke, *Die Sonnete an Orpheus* 6).

The revised second line of the second stanza eschews the limitations of the original's heavily Freudian atmosphere in favor of a more matter of fact, undidactic formulation. Though Auden introduced the verb "need," with its biological and psychological overtones, to good effect in the revised version of the first sonnet, here, in order to escape those overtones, he eliminates the verb for the second time in the poem (the first instance occurring in the second line). The term "left behind" suggests a pioneer spirit of adventure as well as the movement over great distances that it leads to, "the long migration" of the next line. Quite probably the revised line, "At his command they left behind their mothers," could not have been written if "salvation" had remained in the preceding line, for then the comparison, whether serious or ironic, of the adventurer to Christ, who left his mother behind and told his disciples to leave their parents and families and follow him, would have been too obvious.

In the third line of this stanza the imagery gains in distinctness now that the subject of the clause is "their wits," and the verb is "sharpened." This type of revision, involving a shift of focus, so that instead of attention being concentrated upon one subject for several lines it moves from one subject to another, is fairly common throughout the sonnet sequence. Quite often, as it does in this case, the revision involves the elimination of that initial "and" so characteristic of Auden's poetry at the time.

Revision of the fourth line follows the pattern established in the third. Again the serializing initial connective is dropped, and again variety and movement are given to the line by shifting the focus to a new subject, this time "camp-fires." The cumulative effect of these revisions is that instead of a syntactically tame recitation concerning the young, the stanza now provides a shifting focus and active imagery. Thanks to revision of the fourth line, not only do the camp-fires gain added substance by becoming the subject of the coordinate clause, but what the teen-agers learn around these camp-fires takes on added meaning. For the old truism, so familiar we scarcely hear it, "all men are brothers," is replaced by the unsettling and novel "all the horde were brothers," though at the cost of interpolating a rare additional definite article. While the original phrase went by innocuously, this formulation disturbs and demands thought, for the negative associations of "horde" conflict provokingly with the idea of brotherhood. Worn adage is replaced by fertile paradox.

The sestet deals with the hero when, his days of useful glory over, he is forced to linger on, superfluous and miserable. The first line of the sestet is radically changed, the image of a full earth used in the earlier version abandoned and replaced by a coldly literal statement of fact. That efficient, heartless, unpoetic statement, "Till what he came to do was done," achieves several ends. It makes quite clear, first of all, a time and place in history. It also coldly points out that the time is now past and its very coldness, emphasizing the implacability of time, necessity, evolution, or whatever one chooses to call it, provokes in the reader a certain pity for the doomed ex-hero. The earlier version, speaking as it does of the earth being full, tends to obscure matters, for though the fullness of the earth may be consequent upon the hero's deeds, his specific task and accomplishment was not to fill the earth but to open it. He was the leader who pushed back all frontiers, but it was those forces of civilization which followed in his wake that filled the earth. He became "unwanted" not once the earth was full, but before that, as soon as all lands were known and enemies conquered. In the process of revising, Auden has cut down the originally overextended line of thirteen syllables to a comfortably correct eleven.

In the second line of the sestet, Auden drops unneeded connectives and a definite article while replacing a coordinate clause with an efficient participial phrase. "Grew" dropped from line seven, reappears here as the past participial "grown," taking the place of the abandoned clause's subject and verb, "he became." This efficient reworking gives Auden room to elaborate playfully and devastatingly upon the hero's fallen state with a string of colorful and sadly humorous adjectives. Now the obsolescent adventurer appears, with dignity and stature gone, middle-aged and middle-class, in a world without wilderness or romance: "Grown seedy, paunchy, pouchy, and disappointed." The jingly nursery rhyme combination of "paunchy, pouchy," makes the retired hero seem ridiculous and absurd, but the alliterative echo it finds in "disappointed" at the end of the line, mingles with the ridicule a pathos and a sadness. The choice of adjectives in this line proves equally apt for the ex-hero, whether he sinks in desperation to being a low-world murderer or, in greater desperation, to being a bourgeois office worker, the two alternatives that the ensuing lines propose. By eliminating "shabby and demented," Auden pointedly suggests that this sorry spectacle occurs, not off on the Bowery or on Skid Row, but within our own social ranks.

In line eleven, the initial "and" is replaced by "he," a slight grammatical shift necessitated by the conversion of the previous line from a coordinate clause with subject and verb to a participial phrase lacking both. This is the fifth of six instances in this poem in which an initial "and" is discarded.

Revision of the poem's penultimate line adds to it a new dimension. The rather neutral, if not hangdog "spoke approvingly," is replaced by the violently vivid image "Boomed at his children." The verb conveys the frustration and rage of the superannuated hero robbed of his natural function in life. The prepositional phrase reveals to us that he has become a family man, a dull householder instead of the daring leader of young adventurers that he had been. It also implies that the energies that formerly had enabled him to lead, guide, and direct worthy followers, having been deprived of their natural outlet, now reappear in the form of sporadic bursts of rage directed against his unheroic offspring, symbols of his own degeneration and loss. "Law and Order" remain unchanged from the earlier version, watchwords of conservative society that must taste metallic and noxious on the bereft adventurer's tongue. Yet they are the words he must speak, for they are the values that, ironically enough, he himself, through his primitive heroic exploits happily achieved in a lawless world, has helped establish. A hero in a lawless world without order, by his victories he paved the way for civilization and its handmaidens, planting the seeds of his own obsolescence. So we see the misplaced man booming to his unwanted offspring advice, which, by his very nature, he abhors.

The ultimate line, therefore, comes as no shock: "And hated life with heart and soul." The revision in this line, however, seems of questionable worth. For the sake of discarding an inoffensive "all" and gaining an alliterative effect with "hated" and "heart," Auden has introduced an expression, "heart and soul," that one encounters so regularly in the lyrics of popular songs that much of its evocative power is lost.

The extensive revisions in this poem include the elimination of six initial "and's" and five scattered definite articles, the reduction of three capitalized abstractions to lower case modifiers, and a number of grammatical restructurings. The overall effect of the changes is to produce a richer imagery, both more extensive and sharper, a greater poignancy to the poem's irony and paradox, and a happy replacement of jargon and triteness with a particular aptness of detail.

VI (*Journey to War*)

He watched the stars and noted birds in flight;
The rivers flooded or the Empire fell:
He made predictions and was sometimes right;
His lucky guesses were rewarded well.

And fell in love with Truth before he knew her,
And rode into imaginary lands,
With solitude and fasting hoped to woo her,
And mocked at those who served her with their hands.

But her he never wanted to despise,
But listened always for her voice; and when
She beckoned to him, he obeyed in meekness,

And followed her and looked into her eyes;
Saw there reflected every human weakness,
And saw himself as one of many men. (Auden, *Journey* 249–50)

VI *(CSP)*

He watched the stars and noted birds in flight;
A river flooded or a fortress fell:
He made predictions that were sometimes right;
His lucky guesses were rewarded well.

Falling in love with Truth before he knew her,
He rode into imaginary lands,
By solitude and fasting hoped to woo Her,
And mocked at those who served Her with their hands.

Drawn as he was to magic and obliqueness,
In Her he honestly believed, and when
At last She beckoned to him he obeyed,

Looked in Her eyes: awe-struck but unafraid,
Saw there reflected every human weakness,
And knew himself as one of many men. (Auden, *CSP* 130)

Sonnet VI provides the only example of a revised rhyme pattern in "Sonnets from China," with the exception of the concluding poem, "To E.M. Forster." The pattern of the earlier version is ABAB CDCD EFG EGF, that of the revised version ABAB CDCD EFG GEF. Though it appears from a comparison of the two schemes that the change simply involves a switching around of lines twelve and thirteen, this is not the case. In fact, only three lines in the sestet retain their original end words: lines ten, thirteen, and fourteen. The changes undergone by the end words of the sestet are the following:

Becomes:

Line 9	(E) despise	(E) obliqueness
Line 10	(F) when	(F) when
Line 11	(G) meekness	(G) obeyed
Line 12	(E) eyes	(G) unafraid
Line 13	(G) weakness	(E) weakness
Line 14	(F) men	(F) men

As can be seen, only the rhyme pair in lines ten and fourteen, "when-men," remained unchanged.

In the octave all rhymes are full and, with the exception of the feminine endings in lines five and seven, "knew Her-woo Her," all are masculine. In the sestet all endings consist of perfect masculine rhymes except for "meekness-weakness" in the earlier version and "obliqueness-weakness" in the revised version. Throughout the sonnet, lines with masculine endings consist of ten syllables, those with feminine endings sport the conventional eleventh syllable.

Sonnet VI deals with the dedicated man of science, enamored of Truth. His methodical observations of nature and his dabblings and occasional successes in prognosticating are juxtaposed in the first quatrain. His self-righteous, blind and pitiable love affair with Truth is recorded in the second quatrain. The sestet deals with his sudden and shocking enlightenment when, finally, upon boldly looking Truth in the eye, he "Saw there reflected every human weakness, / And he knew himself as one of many men." The quatrains show the early searcher after truth muddling science and magic, ever confident in his own dedication to the Goddess. The tercets show that whatever hocus-pocus he may have dealt in, he was honest in his desire to find Truth, and, when the opportunity arose, he did not flee, but grimly "Looked in Her eyes," and discovered unexpected, sober human truths.

In the octave only line two is substantially revised. It is changed from "The rivers flooded or the Empire fell" to "A river flooded or a fortress fell." Not surprisingly the two definite articles are reduced to indefinite articles. This change, together with the retreat from "the Empire" to "a fortress," brings down to manageable scale the two examples of disaster. It is fairly rare for an Empire to fall, and to squeeze in such a major event quietly between humdrum stargazing and birdwatching on the one, and hit-or-miss soothsaying on the other, is rather heavy-handed irony. Of course the idea of the line is to put our disasters, so apparently overwhelming, into proper perspective, to view them from a great height, in the context of all vast space and time, or at least in the context of all human history. The intent clearly is to suggest the relative unimportance, even the casualness, of these catastrophes. But if the disasters so cavalierly minimized are in our limited human experience of truly enormous import, the effect becomes simply comic and we laugh at its cleverness rather than at man's foolish lack of proportion or vision. So Auden wisely limits the flood, confining it to the river, while tempering the military defeat, reducing it from total overthrow of the Empire to a local loss. The reader understands how these local misfortunes appear to those involved, but at the same time sees how small they are submerged in the general flow of history. Before moving on, it is worth remarking how successful the revision is in terms of sound. The added alliterative effect of "fortress" joining "flooded" and "fell" results in one of the most euphonious lines in the entire sonnet sequence.

The remaining revisions in the octave are relatively minor. Three of them involve the elimination of the connective "and." In line three a simple sentence with a compound predicate is transformed into a compound sentence with an adjective clause, neatly cutting out the deprecated conjunction: "He made predictions and was sometimes right." In lines five and six, Auden manages to eliminate two initial "and's" utilizing a clever and characteristic grammatical trick. The subject of the entire poem has already been established in the first stanza, notably in lines one and three. Though the first stanza ends with a period in both versions, Auden chooses, in the earlier version, to tack on additional descriptive predicates, linking them through initial "and's" to each other and ultimately back to the subject, "He," in line three. In the revised version, however, Auden chooses to begin the second quatrain with a participial phrase, following it with a necessary main clause, thereby discarding both initial connectives. Bearing in mind the subject "He" established in the first quatrain, one easily can follow the grammatical change Auden employs to enable him to vary his sentence structure and avoid the cloying reappearance of initial "and's" in line after line:

> And fell in love with Truth before he knew her,
> And rode into imaginary lands,

Becomes:

> Falling in love with Truth before he knew Her,
> He rode into imaginary lands,

A similar grammatical conversion occurs in the last tercet of Sonnet III, though that case involves a past participle. Auden handily uses this technique for eliminating redundant coordinating conjunctive locutions throughout his revisions of these sonnets.

Another minor revision in the second quatrain is the capitalization of the pronoun that stands for "Truth," namely "her." The pronoun appears in lines five, seven, and eight, and in each instance the lower case of the earlier version is changed to upper. Having decided, apparently, that in this poem the retention of the capitalized, abstract noun, "Truth," was essential to indicate that "She" was worshipped as a Goddess, Auden decided to be consistent and have his pronouns match the upper case of their abstract noun.

The only other revision in the second quatrain, seemingly of little importance, is the change of the initial word in line seven from "With" to "By."

Stanza three is entirely changed. Revision has made it richer, adding a new idea and establishing a paradox. The two versions of the tercet follow:

First Version:

But her he never wanted to despise,
But listened always for her voice; and when
She beckoned to him, he obeyed in meekness,

Revised Version:

Drawn as he was to magic and obliqueness,
In Her he honestly believed, and when
At last She beckoned to him he obeyed

The revised first line reintroduces the idea, touched upon in the opening stanza, of magic, the art of controlling the forces of the universe through binding spells, of compelling events, or at least foreseeing them. Man greatly desires order and control as well as Truth (see sonnet III for the desire for control and order, sonnet I for the desire for Truth), and hopes to achieve them by magical means, but, of course, must ultimately fail. In this tercet, man's attraction to magic as described in the first line jars disturbingly with his belief in and obedience to Truth as presented in the ensuing two lines. It seems incongruous and illogical to the modern reader, who sees "magic and obliqueness" as false paths, that Auden should seem to cite the protagonist's attraction to these methods as evidence of his honest belief in Truth. If my reading of the tercet is correct, and the participial phrase is intended as a kind of confirmatory description of the believer in Truth rather than an elliptical implied contrast with "though" and "yet" omitted, then Auden has confronted us with a thought-provoking, apparently illogical connection. He links a man's interest in magic with his honest belief in Truth, showing us how limited and naïve man is, worshipping the goddess Truth in his heart while performing all her rites falsely. Yet he shows that man to be admirable as well when he dares to look Truth in the eye. The addition of "At last" to the third line of the tercet is helpful, indicating, as it does, the protagonist's long wait for Truth while pursuing false "magic and obliqueness," and reconfirming his honest thirst for her.

The first line of the last stanza is significantly revised. "And followed her and looked into her eyes;" becomes "Looked in Her eyes: awe-struck but unafraid." "And followed her" is dropped as superfluous, since we have already been told that "when / At last She beckoned to him he obeyed." Having eliminated unnecessary stage directions, Auden uses the salvaged half line to elaborate upon the scientist's feelings now that he has finally been recognized by Truth and allowed to look into Her eyes. Though "awe-struck," he is "unafraid" because he has always honestly believed in Her, no matter how misdirected his actual efforts may have been. Of course, what she shows him as a reward for his dedication is his common human condition, the vision of himself like all others, a mere man among men, fallen, weak, and doomed to die.

It is worth noting that two "and's," one of them in the initial position, have been revised out of line twelve. We have already remarked upon the elimination of "and's" in lines three, five and six. In the process of revising the entire third stanza, Auden managed to eliminate two initial conjunctive "but's" as well. In line twelve an appositive construction dispenses with the initial "and," in line nine a participial phrase replaces a coordinate clause with its initial "but," and in line ten a main clause commencing with a prepositional phrase replaces a similar coordinate construction.

In revising this poem Auden has diversified his sentence structure, eliminated five "and's," two initial "but's," and two definite articles, and altered some of his imagery to produce a more effectively ironic, yet touching, portrait.

The revised version of sonnet VI which appears in *Opere Poetiche* differs interestingly from the later version in *CSP*. Though the octaves are almost identical, and the sestet's final two lines faithfully duplicate, in both, the original, the entire first tercet and first line of the last tercet are radically different. Here are the lines in question as they appear in *Opere Poetiche*:

> In Her, though, he believed through all his lies,
> Was always listening for her voice and when
> She beckoned to him, he obeyed in meekness,
> Approached till he could look into her eyes. (Auden, *Opere Poetiche)*

Line one, instead of "magic and obliqueness" in an interestingly ambiguous participial phrase, gives us a statement of the worshipper's belief in Truth, accompanied by an explanatory "through his lies." In *CSP*, as we have seen, the lies materialize as "magic and obliqueness," while the statement of belief is shifted to an efficient second line. Line two, above, a slightly modified version of the original line, eliminates the initial "but" while substituting imperfect for perfect tense. Line three remains identical to the original. The first line of the last stanza, though still modeled on the original, eliminates the initial "and" and concentrates the movements of the pursuit of Truth with the participial "Approached." However, though "Approached" represents a definite acceleration over "followed," it cannot match the radical telescoping of the final version in which "he obeyed" is followed instantly by "Looked in Her eyes," leaving room in the line for the complementing modifiers "awe-struck" and "unafraid."

What we find in examining these four lines is that at the time of *Opere Poetiche* Auden had already introduced a statement of the worshipper's belief in Truth, had enlivened the man's pursuit of his Goddess with the new verb "approach," and had dropped all three initial conjunctions. However, generalized "lies" had gone only partway toward "magic and obliqueness," and the quickened staging of the pursuit fell far short of its ruthless excision in *CSP*, making room for the effective addition of the adjectives "awe-struck" and "unafraid." Clearly Auden was moving toward his final version at the time of *Opere Poetiche*, but some of the most significant steps were yet to be taken.

VII (*Journey to a War*)

He was their servant—some say he was blind—
And moved among their faces and their things;
Their feeling gathered in him like a wind
And sang: they cried—'It is a God that sings'—

And worshipped him and set him up apart,
And made him vain, till he mistook for song
The little tremors of his mind and heart
At each domestic wrong.

Songs came no more: he had to make them.
With what precision was each strophe planned.
He hugged his sorrow like a plot of land,

And walked like an assassin through the town,
And looked at men and did not like them,
But trembled if one passed him with a frown. (Auden, *Journey* 250)

VII (*CSP*)

He was their servant (some say he was blind),
Who moved among their faces and their things:
Their feeling gathered in him like a wind
And sang. They cried 'It is a God that sings,'

And honoured him, a person set apart,
Till he grew vain, mistook for personal song
The petty tremors of his mind or heart
At each domestic wrong.

Lines came to him no more; he had to make them
(With what precision was each strophe planned):
Hugging his gloom as peasants hug their land,

He stalked like an assassin through the town,
And glared at men because he did not like them,
But trembled if one passed him with a frown. (Auden, *CSP* 131)

Sonnet VII has a rhyme pattern of ABAB CDCD EFF GEG. All the end rhymes are masculine with the exception of the unusual rhyme pair in lines nine and thirteen, "make them-like them." This sonnet, like the others, is in iambic pentameter. All lines are decasyllabic except for line eight, which consists of a mere six syllables, and lines nine and thirteen, forming the feminine consonance rhyme pair. These two lines contain nine syllables each before revision, the standard eleven syllables after revision. All the masculine end-rhymes are perfect, but the rhyme in lines one and three is one of the few eye rhymes in "Sonnets from China," "blind-wind."

This sonnet describes the evolution of the poet. He begins as a blind seer, a singer of revealed truth, a revered poet-prophet, then, honored to excess and victim of his own vanity, he descends to the unhappy state of uninspired growling artisan who, struggling grimly with his mind to form each line of verse, now distrusts and dislikes the fellow man of whom and for whom he used to sing. No longer does he feel that his experiences are those of his fellow men. This poem, in tracing the unhappy evolution of one of civilization's oldest and most important callings, parallels with its depressing development, which is really a degeneration, the movement of several of the other early sonnets, notably III, V, and VIII. It seems clear that many of the sonnets in this sequence recreate or reenact in varied specific guises the original fall dealt with in sonnets I and II, illustrating with the particular the effect of the universal. This sonnet sequence, we should remember, was originally entitled "In Time of War," and was inspired by Auden's experiences as an observer of the Indo-Japanese struggle that was one of the forerunners of World War II. This war, and all others as well, are, of course, prime reminders of our first progenitors' legendary transgression. As Monroe K. Spears says: "This particular war calls up all human failures, which are all, essentially, failures to achieve the truly human" (Spears, *W.H. Auden* 132).

In the first line of the revised version, a parenthesis has taken the place of dashes. Though Auden never used parentheses in "In Time of War," *CSP* reveals three instances of their use, two in this poem and one in sonnet XIV, formerly XVII. In this poem, since the parentheses of the first line replaces dashes, there is no change in intent of great significance, but rather a shift in symbol, perhaps implying a slightly greater separation of the material set off from the body of the verse. In the case of line ten, however, the parenthesis is simply added, though one might remark that the line always lent itself to a parenthetical reading.

In line two an initial "and" is removed in favor of the relative pronoun "who." This not unexpected revision converts the second line from part of a compound predicate to an adjectival subordinate clause, but in no way affects the meaning. This elimination of an initial conjunctive "and" is one of three such cases in this sonnet. In addition, three other uses of "and," not in initial positions, are discarded.

The first line of the second quatrain is significantly revised: "And worshipped him and set him apart," becomes "And honoured him, a person set apart." Apparently, the implications of the verb in the earlier version went beyond what Auden intended, in any case struck him as misleading upon later rereading. The change of verb is accompanied by an appropriate revision in the following line, a revision of "And made him vain" to "Till he grew vain," indicating quite plainly that Auden felt his earlier version was false in suggesting that the poet had no free will and no responsibility for his own fate. If the people "worshipped" him, they were the sinners and the cause of his downfall. If they merely "honoured" him, they were behaving quite acceptably, and the guilt for his vanity remains clearly his own. This shift of verb is accompanied by a subtle grammatical change that again minimizes the responsibility of the people for their poet's downfall: if they not only "worshipped him" but also deliberately "set him up apart," it seems fair enough to say that they "made him vain." But if they only "honoured him" as someone who seemed to them already "a person set apart" by grace of God, then we are more likely to blame him for the fact that "he grew vain." This revision is only one of several in the sonnet sequence that clearly reveals Auden's insistence upon the individual's freedom and his responsibility.

The next line, as already indicated, is significantly revised as well. "And made him vain, till he mistook for song" now reads, "Till he grew vain, mistook for personal song." As already noted, the deterministic atmosphere of the earlier version, with its implication of a cause-and-effect relationship between the people's worship and the poet's vanity, is gone. Gone too, on the technical level, is another initial "and." The poet's song is now "personal," the modifier focusing attention on the diminishing stature and scope of the poet as he degenerates from prophet to crotchety complainer. His song is no longer of the nation, "their faces and their things," and no longer is "The feeling gathered in him like a wind," for now his vision encompasses only his own trivial affairs. The ironic force of the term "personal song" depends largely upon the descriptive passages that follow in the next two lines. These lines remain largely unchanged, the only noteworthy revision being the substitution of "petty tremors" for "little tremors." This revision provides yet another example of Auden's attention to connotation and nuance. The word "petty" implies a smallness of character that is most appropriate since the whole quatrain is concerned with the hubristic descent and degeneration of the ex-vates. The only other revision in the line is the conversion of an "and" to an "or."

The revisions of the second quatrain all work together to focus attention upon the poet himself, casting the burden of responsibility for his fate squarely upon his own shoulders, while emphasizing his pathetic diminution in stature and spirit.

The first line of the sestet, "Songs came no more," becomes "Lines came to him no more." The repetition of the word song which has already appeared in varied forms three times in the poem is avoided. The change also shifts attention to the actual structure of poetry, preparing us for the image that the next verse presents of laborious planning in the construction of a poem. The explanatory "to him" conveniently fills in the syllabic count, increasing it from nine to the conventional eleven Auden used in almost all lines with a feminine ending.

The following line remains unchanged but is placed within parentheses. The interpolation seems reasonable enough, for the line, a tour de force epitomizing precise planning—with three alliterating *w*'s, three *s* sounds, and two alliterating *p*'s—is somewhat disconnected from those that precede and follow it.

The third line of the first tercet is changed from "He hugged his sorrow like a plot of land" to "Hugging his gloom as peasants hug their land." The syntactic change to a participial phrase serves conveniently to allow the elimination of an initial "and" in the following line, as the subject "he," making a slightly delayed entrance, replaces the conjunction. This reliance upon the participial phrase for variety of sentence structure and elimination of hypnotic repetitive "and's" has already been demonstrated in numerous instances throughout the earlier sonnets. Personal "sorrow" seems to be more suggestive of universal suffering and the plight of the human condition than personal "gloom," which always seems somehow self-created, self-imposed and even selfish. The phrase "Hugging his gloom" reminds one rather of a child self-indulgently immersing himself in the sulks. This revision parallels in direction the changes in the second quatrain, particularly the replacement of "little" with "petty." The poet's pathetic diminution to a solipsistic, dissatisfied, misanthropic loner gains added force from the introduction of words that paint an image of unhappy decayed narcissism.

However, the greatest improvement in this line is the elimination of a typical elliptical and puzzling simile and its replacement by a logical and sensibly direct reformulation. How can the reader guess what is it like to hug a plot of land? Do poets hug lots of land, and if so with what emotions? The obscure becomes clear with revision, for now Auden fills in the missing essential element of the analogy. Our friend from sonnet IV, the peasant, squeezed out of the overly concise original simile, is reintroduced in the revised version, and explains it all. A peasant has nothing but his bit of land and clings to it accordingly with passion; the declining poet, we now understand, has nothing left but his gloom, to which he clings as the last vestige of human emotion, distorted remnant that it is.

A simile involving relationships, such as the one just analyzed, might be diagramed as A is to B as C is to D. In such a compound simile there is always the temptation to leave out element C, hoping or assuming that it will be understood. But since the reader is really concerned with A, what I. A. Richards calls the tenor, and since C has played no part at all in the poem, it is quite unlikely that he will guess correctly at the missing term unless its relationship to D is so traditionally established that the mention of one automatically calls to mind the other. In general the reader will assume, in the absence of C, that the simile should read A is to B as A is to D. In the above example the reader would assume that the poet "hugged his sorrow" the way he hugged a plot of land and would be mystified. It would seem that element C can be safely omitted only when it might stand for all men, including A himself. For example, if one said, "He hugged his sorrow like a million dollars," everyone would understand, for the implications of the term "a million dollars" are quite clear to all of us, whether we be capitalist, communist, or mendicant friar. Auden's verse of the late thirties contains a number of elliptical similes such as the one just analyzed, but revision has eliminated many of them.

In the last stanza the first words are changed from "And walked" to "He stalked." The initial conjunction is eliminated and the general, unevocative verb "walked" is replaced by a verb carrying the suggestion of a stiffness born of pride and fear. In the next line "looked" becomes "glared," again the general and merely denotative becoming the specific and connotative. In this same line an "and" becomes "because he," the change achieving the elimination of yet another "and" while introducing a causal relationship between the manner of looking at the townsmen and the poet's dislike of them. "Because" gives us a meaningful connection, "and" a merely grammatical one.

A number of punctuation changes in this sonnet, in addition to the introduction of parenthesis, are worth mentioning. In the last line of the first stanza a colon becomes a period and the dashes surrounding a quotation are dropped: "And sang: they cried—'It is a God that sings'—" becomes "And sang. They cried 'It is a God that sings.'" Both changes are healthy. The period is emphatic and clean, as well as more logical than the colon. The dashes around the quotation are superfluous and confusing and their elimination makes the line more readable. In line ten, a final period is replaced by a colon, a change that seems ill-advised, since what follows the colon is not in apposition with what precedes it. In line two a semicolon becomes a colon (though not in *Opere Poetiche*), and in line nine the reverse occurs, neither revision affecting the poem to any great extent. Line four sees a final comma added, line nine a period dropped.

VIII (*Journey to a War*)

He turned his field into a meeting-place,
And grew the tolerant ironic eye,
And formed the mobile money-changer's face,
And found the notion of equality.

And strangers were as brothers to his clocks,
And with his spires he made a human sky;
Museums stored his learning like a box,
And paper watched his money like a spy.

It grew so fast his life was overgrown,
And he forgot what once it had been made for,
And gathered into crowds and was alone,

And lived expensively and did without,
And could not find the earth which he had paid for,
Nor feel the love that he knew all about. (Auden, *Journey* 250–51)

VIII (*CSP*)

He turned his field into a meeting-place,
Evolved a tolerant ironic eye,
Put on a mobile money-changer's face,
Took up the doctrine of Equality.

Strangers were hailed as brothers by his clocks,
With roof and spire he built a human sky,
Stored random facts in a museum box,
To watch his treasure set a paper spy.

All grew so fast his life was overgrown,
Till he forgot what all had once been made for:
He gathered into crowds but was alone,

And lived expensively but did without,
No more could touch the earth which he had paid for,
Nor feel the love which he knew all about. (Auden, *CSP* 131)

Sonnet VIII has a rhyme scheme of ABAB CDCD EFE GFG, the same pattern as that of sonnet II. With three exceptions, the lines have masculine endings. Lines ten and thirteen end in the feminine rhymes "made for" and "paid for," while line four ends with the word "equality," a heavy stress falling on the second syllable, a secondary stress on the last. "Equality" provides a kind of rhyme for "eye" in line two, reminiscent of Emily Dickinson's practice of rhyming such words as *tree* and *die* or *day* and *eternity*. Babette Deutsch, in her *Poetry Handbook*, calls this relatively rare device "in which any vowel is allowed to agree with any other," a vowel rhyme. (Deutsch, *Poetry Handbook* 125). The sonnet is in iambic pentameter, the meter that dominates the entire sonnet sequence. The two lines with feminine endings add, of course, an expected eleventh syllable.

This sonnet deals with the overall rapid development of western civilization, a growth marked by a burgeoning of ideas such as "the doctrine of Equality," the evolution of "a tolerant ironic eye," the growth of international commerce, the expansion of cities and their industries, the accumulation of and interest in mere facts, and the invention of paper currency to facilitate trade. The octave notes these signs of raging progress while the sestet, commenting that "All grew so fast his life was overgrown," shows how man's endeavors ran away from him, depriving him of all primal joy—friendship, love, the feel of the earth—and leaving him alone in vast crowds, with plenty of money and little happiness. In depicting man's general enslavement to his own ideas, activities, and things, accompanied by a gradual loss of nature and the natural, this poem elaborates upon themes already introduced in sonnets III, IV, and V.

Revision of sonnet VIII is primarily an exercise in eliminating recurrent initial "and's" while giving to the poem a greater variety in syntactical patterns. Of the ten lines which, in the original version, begin with the enumerative connective, only one retains it in *CSP*. Most of the omissions are accomplished quite simply, as in the first quatrain where all three initial "and's" are neatly and effectively dropped. Comparing the two versions of the poem one finds that the connectives served no necessary grammatical function, and that, by simply dropping them, Auden gains an extra syllable to play with in each line. Though a number of later revisions entail the use of prepositional phrases, most are accomplished as simply as those of the first quatrain, demanding no grammatical or syntactical rearrangements.

In the second line of the first quatrain, "And grew the" becomes "Evolved a," introducing the idea of serious, long-term historical changes that are slow but sure, and replacing the proscribed definite article with an indefinite one. In the next line the same type of revision occurs, "And formed the" becoming "Put on a." The new verb, by implying volition and free choice, suggests that the "money-changer's face" is a willed mask and those who put it on are responsible for their action. This new implication with its somber overtones of guilt replaces a basically neutral, unsuggestive, merely denotative formulation. This revision seems to function along the same lines as those in the much revised second stanza of sonnet VII, discussed above.

In the last line of the first quatrain revision is extensive. "And found the notion of equality" becomes "Took up the doctrine of Equality." Again, the initial "and" is dropped, though this time the object's article is allowed to remain definite. The change in verb is worth examining, for it does more than follow the pattern of the new verb with its accompanying preposition in the previous line. "Took up" suggests a similar facility and falseness to that suggested by "Put on." It is a term redolent of casualness and dilettantism, suggesting in conjunction with serious ideas a certain nonchalance and carelessness and ultimate lack of sincerity or interest. When the direct object of this expression is an abstraction or a concept or system, the intent of the writer is almost always to cast an ironic and critical light upon the verb's frivolous subject. So, in the present context, the implication is that the evolving western man is approaching serious matters superficially, without thought, feeling, or honesty. Auden apparently relied on the word "notion" to carry his implied criticism in the earlier version, but upon changing the verb he likely felt that the point was clear enough and accordingly dropped the noun with its suggestion of weakness and instability in favor of the staunch and definite "doctrine." The more serious the connotations of "doctrine" are, the more pointed is the criticism implied by the expression "Took up."

The first line of the second quatrain is revised from "And strangers were as brothers to his clocks" to "Strangers were hailed as brothers by his clocks." A needless conjunction is dropped and a copulative verb is replaced by the passive voice of a transitive verb whose optimistic and hearty overtones fit well with the illusory feeling of ultimate success and achievement prevalent during a period of such progress and prosperity.

The following line is revised from "And with his spires he made a human sky" to "With roof and spire he built a human sky." The initial "and" is gone, though the line now uses the conjunction elsewhere. The "human sky" is more cluttered and more human, containing not only church spires but the roofs of human domiciles as well. Together, "roof and spire" do compose a truly human, man-made sky, "spire" alone a picturesque but partial view. The change in verb follows a pattern already noted several times in earlier sonnets of replacing a general, abstract, merely denotative, unevocative verb with a more specific, concrete, and palpable verb that carries with it overtones or connotations that may arouse the imagination. "He built" suggests labor, effort, achievement, perhaps even wood, stone, cement, carpentry and mason work. "He made" simply tells us that man-made spires fill the sky, but it does not suggest the reality of their construction, neither man's sweat nor the material he used.

The third line of the second quatrain, originally "Museums stored his learning like a box," now reads "Stored random facts in a museum box." "His learning" is reduced to "random facts" in accordance with the drift of the revisions throughout this poem. A substantive with generally positive connotations is replaced by a much more specific image with largely negative connotations. That man's great success is an illusion is the burden of the sestet, so it seems logical to describe, in the octave, his varied activities in terms that hint at the ultimate hollowness of his achievement. The revised line reduces man's intellectual endeavors to another form of material acquisition, for it describes his intellectual progress in terms of the accumulation and safe-depositing of random facts. Facts being stored in boxes is depressing enough, but the modifier makes man's futility flagrant, for the suggestion is that he records and preserves without trying to order, correlate, and understand. In revising this line Auden has again cut one of those facile similes whose automatic appearances were so characteristic of his verse in the late thirties. In this instance he replaces the simile with a symbolic direct statement avoiding all tropes. Monroe K. Spears refers to Auden's former practices as "the vice of over-facility, of making tricks of style mechanical," and gives as examples two lines from sonnet XX, a sonnet which Auden has now discarded from the sequence (Spears, *W.H. Auden* 156).

The last line of the second quatrain, originally "And paper watched his money like a spy," now reads "To watch his treasure set a paper spy." Another initial conjunction is eliminated and another facile simile as well. It seems clear that Auden feels he overused that simile, often neglecting logical coherence in the pursuit of elliptical conciseness. The revised line retains the verb "watch," but the syntactical shift has made man (understood) the subject, "spy" the object, "paper" a modifier of "spy," and the infinitive "to watch" a verbal with "spy" for its subject and "treasure" for its object. The change of "money" to "treasure" is an improvement since money already suggests paper currency to the modern reader, destroying the effectiveness of the image in the earlier version. It seems, in spite of all these changes, that the meaning of the line has not really changed: paper currency replaces precious objects as man tries to control and facilitate exchange and trade through establishment of an arbitrary, artificial, consistent monetary standard. It is worth noting that the revised line has gained an alliterative effect in "set a paper spy" which nicely echoes the *s* sound recurrent throughout the stanza, a consonantal hiss appearing five times in the first line, twice in the second, and thrice in the third.

Revision in the sestet is less extensive than in the octave. In the first tercet three "and's" are dropped, two of them in the initial position. The first is replaced by the preposition "till," the second, thanks to the replacement of a comma with a colon at the end of line ten, with the subject "he," and the third by the more exact and appropriate conjunction "but." The vague pronoun "it," clearly without any antecedent in the entire poem, is replaced in lines nine and ten by the expansive pronoun "all," so all-encompassing that its meaning, equivalent to that of "everything," is quite clear without any antecedent. The implied noun is "things," and it might be more sensible to look at "all" as an adjective for the understood "things." In line ten the change of "it" to "all" is accompanied by a slight rearrangement in the word order, improving the flow of the verse: "And he forgot what once it had been made for" becomes "Till he forgot what all had once been made for."

In the first line of the last stanza the initial "and" is retained, but a second one is replaced by a more appropriate "but." "And," conveying a relationship of addition, is hardly the proper connective to place between "lived expensively" and "did without;" "but," conveying a relationship of contrast, is, of course, just right.

In the next line, "And could not find" becomes "No more could touch." Again an initial "and" is discarded, this time in favor of a negative construction that suits well the melancholy or pathos of the line. The change in the verb involves, typically, a movement from concept to experience, from abstract to specific, from a word of the mind to one of the senses, of the body. The tactile verb "touch" is true to lived experience, for quite literally the city dweller is separated from the earth, for which he has paid, by cobble stones, wooden floors, and cement. The verb "find," if pursued, may evoke a silly image of a man running around looking for his lost soil as if it were a lost key. If not pursued, it may evoke some vague sentiment perhaps, but no image whatsoever.

IX (*Journey to a War*)

> They died and entered the closed life like nuns:
> Even the very poor lost something; oppression
> Was no more a fact; and the self-centered ones
> Took up an even more extreme position.

And the kingly and the saintly also were
Distributed among the woods and oceans,
And touch our open sorrow everywhere,
Airs, waters, places, round our sex and reasons;

Are what we feed on as we make our choice.
We bring them back with promises to free them,
But as ourselves continually betray them:

They hear their deaths lamented in our voice,
But in our knowledge know we could restore them;
They could return to freedom; they would rejoice. (Auden, *Journey to a War*)

X (*Journey to a War*)

As a young child the wisest could adore him;
He felt familiar to them like their wives:
The very poor saved up their pennies for him,
And martyrs brought him presents of their lives.

But who could sit and play with him all day?
Their other needs were pressing, work, and bed:
The beautiful stone courts were built where they
Could leave him to be worshipped and well fed.

But he escaped. They were too blind to tell
That it was he who came with them to labour,
And talked and grew up with them like a neighbour:

To fear and greed those courts became a centre;
The poor saw there the tyrant's citadel,
And martyrs the lost face of the tormentor. (Auden, *Journey to a War*)

Sonnets IX and X from "In Time of War" are dropped from the sequence as it appears in *CSP*. Perhaps Auden felt that the essence of what he was attempting to convey in sonnet IX was presented with greater clarity and effect in sonnet XX of *CSP*. As for sonnet X, he says, "I dropped it because I thought a specifically Christian theme was out of place in the Sequence" (Letter to A.L., Sept. 8, 1971). One might add that *CSP*'s sonnet IX, using different imagery, deals with the same theme, the misuse of God's messenger and of his message.

XI (*Journey to a War*)

He looked in all His wisdom from the throne
Down on the humble boy who kept the sheep,
And sent a dove; the dove returned alone:
Youth liked the music, but soon fell asleep.

But He had planned such future for the youth:
Surely His duty now was to compel;
For later he would come to love the truth,
And own his gratitude. The eagle fell.

It did not work: his conversation bored
The boy who yawned and whistled and made faces,
And wriggled free from fatherly embraces;

But with the eagle he was always willing
To go where it suggested, and adored
And learnt from it the many ways of killing. (Auden, *Journey to a War* 251)

IX *(CSP)*

He looked in all His wisdom from His throne
Down on the humble boy who herded sheep,
And sent a dove. The dove returned alone:

Song put a charmed rusticity to sleep.
But He had planned such future for this youth:
Surely, His duty now was to compel,
To count on time to bring true love of truth
And, with it, gratitude. His eagle fell.

It did not work: His conversation bored
The boy, who yawned and whistled and made faces,
And wriggled free from fatherly embraces,

But with His messenger was always willing
To go where it suggested, and adored,
And learned from it so many ways of killing. (Auden, *CSP* 132)

Sonnet XI from "In Time of War" appears as sonnet IX in *CSP*. It has a rhyme scheme of ABAB CDCD EFF GEG, a pattern that has appeared already in sonnet VII and will appear again in sonnet XVII. There are two feminine rhyme pairs, "faces-embraces" and "willing-killing." All other endings consist of perfect masculine rhymes. The meter is iambic pentameter, the lines all decasyllabic save those with feminine endings, all of which exhibit a characteristic eleventh syllable.

This sonnet concerns the relationship between God and man, with the role of the church undergoing serious scrutiny at the same time. Man, destined for great things, is called by God's messenger, the dove, but its song of peace only lulls him to sleep. God then sends the eagle to awaken man and bring him to his Lord, but man finds God's conversation boring, and, like a child, wriggles "free from fatherly embraces." However, though put to sleep by the dove and bored by God Himself, man is entranced by the eagle and follows this messenger into many false paths. The eagle, borrowed from the legend of Zeus and Ganymede, in which Zeus sends down an eagle to kidnap the beautiful youth and bring him back to serve as Zeus' cupbearer, seems clearly enough to represent, in this poem, the church militant and that spirit of worldly conquest and triumph by fire and destruction which was no small part of the church's development. The poem, depicting man's indifference to God and his messenger of peace and avid acceptance of his fierce messenger of war, is applicable, of course, to almost all of western history, but may suggest, in particular, those perversions of Christianity such as the Crusades and the Inquisition.

Though only two lines in sonnet IX have been thoroughly reworked, there are a fair number of minor revisions, many involving the elimination or replacement of a definite article. In the first line of the poem, "the throne" is revised to "His throne," the first of eight instances in this sonnet in which the definite article is dropped. In the second line, "who kept the sheep" becomes "who herded sheep." Another "the" is dropped and a specific literal verb replaces one that is general and abstract. The conversion of a semicolon to a period in line three results in a deepened pause before the start of a new sentence, affording the image of the unsuccessful dove a sharpness and emphasis it had previously lacked: "And sent a dove. The dove returned alone."

The last line of the first quatrain is substantially revised. "Youth liked the music, but soon fell asleep" becomes "Song put a charmed rusticity to sleep." As in sonnet V, where revision introduced "teen-agers" into the poem, the word "youth" has again been replaced by a word with more pointed suggestiveness. "Rusticity" calls forth an image of gawkish naivety that explains and even endears the foolish youth to the reader. The elimination of the word "youth" does away with the rather weak repetition of that word in lines four and five of the original. In the process of being revised, the line has also lost its definite article, the third such cut in the first quatrain.

Though the revised line has a smoothness and polish that elegantly conveys the feeling of the charming song, I prefer the clean simplicity and directness of expression in the earlier version. The introduction of a four-syllable word, "rusticity," employed in an unfamiliar way and accompanied by another Latin derivative for a modifier, all in place of a simple, monosyllabic Anglo-Saxon word, swings the focus of attention away from the natural and simple boy and towards the effectiveness of the complex and artificial song instead. In addition, subject and object have been reversed, so that the line now begins with the subject "Song" in place of "Youth," thus further assisting the shift in focus.

In the first line of the second quatrain "the youth" becomes "this youth." In the second line a comma is inserted after "Surely," and the semicolon at the end of the line is reduced to a comma. Line three is substantially rewritten. "For later he would come to love the truth" becomes "To count on time to bring true love of truth." Instead of shifting focus to man, the revised line retains "His duty" as subject of the sentence in which this infinitive phrase forms a predicate complement. The emotional effectiveness of the revision comes from the phrase "true love of truth," with its deceptive simplicity of language, and its childish repetition of the same word as adjective, then abstract noun. By its own innocent formulation, this phrase conveys a sense of the utter simplicity and purity of truth itself. It is worth remarking that revision has replaced the alliteration of "*l*ater he would come to *l*ove" with a barrage of t's: "*T*o coun*t* on *t*ime *t*o bring *t*rue love of *t*ruth." Revision has also eliminated one more definite article.

The last line of the second quatrain is changed from "And own his gratitude. The eagle fell." to "And, with it, gratitude. His eagle fell." The first half of the line is changed for grammatical reasons necessitated by the revision of the previous line. The abrupt sentence composing the second half of the line merely loses a definite article in favor of the possessive pronoun. This minor revision may be helpful in making clear that the eagle is God's own messenger, therefore making more ironic the tragic misuse man makes of it.

The first tercet of the sestet has only minor changes: "his conversation" becomes "His conversation" to make clear that it is God and not the eagle who bores the boy, a comma is inserted after "The boy" in the second line, and the third line's terminal semicolon is reduced to a comma, allowing the pronoun "he" to be dropped from the following line.

In the first line of the last stanza "the eagle" becomes "His messenger," while the now unnecessary "he" is dropped to make room for the added syllable in messenger: "But with the eagle he was always willing" becomes "But with His messenger was always willing." There may have been some obscurity about the eagle, so suddenly introduced at the tail end of the second stanza, so, instead of repeating the symbol, Auden chooses to name it by its function. The point becomes perhaps a bit clearer—bored by his Father's conversation, the youth is charmed enough by the messenger itself, presumably the Church militant, so that he will follow it anywhere, without thought or understanding, and, in the process, will learn evil instead of good.

The remaining changes in the poem are minor. A comma is affixed to the end of the penultimate line, "learnt" is Americanized to "learned," and "the many ways of killing" loses its definite article in favor of "so." This final revision seems a mistake. Occasionally, in his efforts to obliterate all signs of his former penchant for the definite article, Auden will discard a most effective "the." In this case it seems clear that the quiet understatement of the original version is far more effective in a chillingly controlled and undramatic fashion than is the revised version with its emotional adverb "so."

In general I have tried to show that Auden's revisions give an added life, depth, and suggestiveness to these sonnets. In the case of sonnet IX, I suspect that the original version, whatever minor shortcomings it may have, is more effective emotionally, and maybe even intellectually, than it is in its revised form.

XII (*Journey to a War*)

And the age ended, and the last deliverer died
In bed, grown idle and unhappy; they were safe:
The sudden shadow of the giant's enormous calf
Would fall no more at dusk across the lawn outside.

They slept in peace: in marshes here and there no doubt
A sterile dragon lingered to a natural death,
But in a year the spoor had vanished from the heath;
The kobold's knocking in the mountain petered out.

Only the sculptors and the poets were half sad,
And the pert retinue from the magician's house
Grumbled and went elsewhere. The vanquished powers were glad

To be invisible and free: without remorse
Struck down the sons who strayed into their course,
And ravished the daughters, and drove the fathers mad. (Auden,
Journey to a War 252)

X (*CSP*)

So an age ended and its last deliverer died
In bed, grown idle and unhappy; they were safe:
The sudden shadow of a giant's enormous calf
Would fall no more at dusk across their lawn outside.

They slept in peace: in Marshes here and there no doubt
A sterile dragon lingered to a natural death,
But in a year the slot had vanished from the heath;
A kobold's knocking in the mountain petered out.

Only the poets and the sculptors were half-sad,
And the pert retinue from the magician's house
Grumbled and went elsewhere. The vanquished powers were glad

To be invisible and free; without remorse
Struck down the silly sons who strayed into their course,
And ravished the daughters, and drove the fathers mad. (Auden,
CSP 132)

CSP's sonnet X (formerly sonnet XII) manifests a great number of anomalies that are particularly unexpected in a sonnet sequence of a generally conservative nature, a sequence characterized by the use of conventional iambic pentameter lines terminating, for the most part, in perfect rhymes. Sonnet X is not in iambic pentameter, not all of its lines end in perfect rhymes, and one end word has no related end word in any other line but finds echoes in the ante-penultimate word of the line immediately following it. One might diagram the rhyme scheme as ABBA CDDC EFE GGE. The octave presents few problems, the enclosing rhymes of both quatrains consisting of perfect masculine endings, the enclosed rhyme pairs consisting of a consonance rhyme in the first quatrain, "safe-calf," and an eye rhyme, "death-heath," that could be called an example of consonance as well, in the second quatrain. The sestet is quite atypical, however. Line two of the first tercet ends with "house," but the only end words that can even be considered as possible rhymes are the rather distantly consonantal rhyme pair of the last stanza, "remorse-course." If one were to accept the presence of a final *s* sound as sufficient agreement to establish the consonance of these three words, our sestet rhyme pattern would become EGE FFE. However a less distant rhyme for "house" is provided by the assonantal (as well as weakly consonantal) "powers" appearing two words from the end of line eleven. Since in all published versions "powers," in fact, stands at the end of the printed line, the concluding words, for lack of space, appearing indented one line below, definite attention is conveniently called to this internal assonance.

The meter of sonnet X is loosely iambic, but the lines contain either six feet or five, following no discernible pattern in their choice. Most lines contain twelve or thirteen syllables, but one line in the original version, the penultimate of the poem, is decasyllabic and in perfect iambic pentameter. Many of the other lines are Alexandrines, but a number, notably lines one, ten, and fourteen, display anapests (with one dactyl in line ten) that reduce the feet to five. All of the second quatrain, however, is composed of regular Alexandrines. This sonnet, together with sonnet XI, marks the point of greatest metrical irregularity in this sequence of, for the most part, conventionally structured sonnets.

Sonnet X deals with the loss of belief, what some might call superstition, consequent upon the general discovery, exploration, and apparent subjugation and civilization of the remaining unknown dark regions of the world. Having relegated all his hideous enemies to mythologies and fairy tales, civilized man "slept in peace," and "only the sculptors and the poets were half sad," deprived of the reality so congenial to their receptive imaginations. Of course ceasing to believe in giants and dragons does not banish evil from the world. Man's confident disbelief proved a great foolishness, for when he convinced himself that the evil beings did not really exist, "The vanquished powers were glad / To be invisible and free," and took a greater toll on him than they had been able to when he still recognized them. Here we see how man, by locking his incarnated enemies into folklorist's archives and children's bedrooms, leaves himself more vulnerable than ever to the forces of evil whose existence he now so lightheartedly denies.

There are scarcely any revisions in this sonnet. The only changes in the first quatrain involve the elimination of definite articles. The opening statement, "And the age ended," becomes "So an age ended," eliminating both the initial "and" and the definite article. Further definite articles are dropped as "the last deliverer" becomes "its last deliverer," the third line's "the giant" becomes "a giant," and the fourth line's "the lawn" becomes "their lawn." All these changes promote a shift from the prototypic to the particular, one could say from the mythic to the historic. However, as we will see, in the last three and a half lines, with definite articles rampant, the mythic quality chillingly reinstates itself.

In the second stanza "spoor" becomes "slot," Auden favoring the more technical hunting term which is also the less familiar word. Perhaps the alien and rare word with its medieval etymology seemed to him more correct for dealing with dragons, a disappearing race. However, *spoor*, though but an early-nineteenth-century Boer word, has, to my ear, an appropriately heavy sound, and I can sympathize with Whitehead when he grumbles, "it seems

pedantic to change the dragon's 'spoor' to the more technical 'slot,' . . . "
(Whitehead, "Vin Audenaire" 492). In the last line of the stanza "The kobold"
becomes, unhappily, to my mind, "A kobold.."

In the third stanza a hyphen is added to "half sad." In the last stanza, the
second line, in perfect iambic pentameter in the earlier version, interpolates
the adjective "silly" into the revised version, adding an extra iambic foot to
result in a perfect Alexandrine, thus matching the previous line with which it
rhymes. The added word alliterates nicely with the *s* sound that dominates the
line: "*S*truck down the *s*illy *s*ons who *s*trayed into their cour*s*e."

Though in the octave five out of nine definite articles are eliminated, all
eight appearing in the sestet remain untouched. Alluding to this disparity,
Auden says: "My feeling about (the definite article's) proper use is . . . well
demonstrated by my use and omission of them in sonnet X... ." (Auden,
Letter to A.L., Sept. 8, 1971). Of those retained in the sestet, the ones in "the
pert retinue" and "the magician's house" seem more grammatically logical
than any substitutions could have been. In "The vanquished powers," the
definite article serves well to convey a sense of the vast, shadowy dimensions, while intimating the permanence of these evil forces. Their strength
and pervasiveness is further suggested by the fact that their victims also retain
the definite article, universalizing the triumph of the inimical in a mythic formulation. However, in the case of "the sculptors and the poets," Auden could
easily have dropped the definite articles in favor of more helpful modifiers,
as so often is his practice.

XIII (*Journey to a War*)

Certainly praise: let the song mount again and again
For life as it blossoms out in a jar or a face,
For the vegetable patience, the animal grace;
Some people have been happy; there have been great men.

But hear the morning's injured weeping and know why:
Cities and men have fallen; the will of the Unjust
Has never lost its power; still, all princes must
Employ the Fairly-Noble unifying Lie.

History opposes its grief to our buoyant song:
The Good Place has not been; our star has warmed to birth
A race of promise that has never proved its worth;

The quick new West is false; and prodigious but wrong
This passive flower-like people who for so long
In the Eighteen Provinces have constructed the earth. (Auden,
Journey to a War 252–53)

XI (*CSP*)

Certainly praise: let song mount again and again
For life as it blossoms out in a jar or a face,
For vegetal patience, for animal courage and grace:
Some have been happy; some, even, were great men.

But hear the morning's injured weeping and know why:
Ramparts and souls have fallen; the will of the unjust
Has never lacked an engine; still all princes must
Employ the fairly-noble unifying lie.

History opposes its grief to our buoyant song,
To our hope its warning. One star has warmed to birth
One puzzled species that has yet to prove its worth:

The quick new West is false, and prodigious but wrong
The flower-like Hundred Families who for so long
In the Eighteen Provinces have modified the earth. (Auden,
CSP 133)

Sonnet XI (formerly XIII) has a rhyme scheme of ABBA CDDC EFF EEF. All the rhymes are masculine. The meter, generally like that in sonnet X, is characterized by lines of five or six feet, usually containing twelve or thirteen syllables. Though many lines are Alexandrines, there are some marked exceptions, such as the anapestic tetrameter of line three and the deliberately free rhythms of line four.

Whereas all the earlier sonnets depict, in one form or another, man's failures and his fall, this sonnet marks a kind of balancing point, striking a note of poised equilibrium in which the yea and the nay, good and evil, joy and sorrow, hope and doubt, appear as the complementary elements of a complex reality. The poem begins with the encouraging "Certainly praise," then admonishes, "But hear the morning's injured weeping and know why." Later on it restates the dichotomy of life: "History opposes its grief to our buoyant song." Though it does not end in a shower of optimism, there seems to be a suggestion of cautious hope in the line "One puzzled species that has yet to prove its worth," the hope arising from the presence of that ambiguous word, "yet." The poem ends with a resolute rejection of the paths taken until now by both "the quick new West" and the "prodigious . . . flower-like Hundred Families" of China. Materialistic, technological progress with its accompanying rejection of the spirit is found to be false, but so is the passive, anti-materialistic, anti-technological, anti-progress spirituality. Both East and West have failed so far, but there is still the future.

John Fuller, in his *Reader's Guide to W.H. Auden*, having arrived at this sonnet, quickly surveys the sequence's overall structure: "At this point the historical preamble is really over. Man is now at a stage of civilization at which consciousness of his failure to create a just society is equally mixed with his hope that he may eventually do so (No. XI). This opposition of admonitory 'history' to the 'buoyant song' of art or love becomes the underlying theme of the remaining sonnets, which now turn to the actual situation in China" (Fuller, *Reader's Guide* 126).

The general pattern that Fuller describes seems to me quite accurate. However, although I think he is reasonable in calling the first half of the sonnet sequence an "historical preamble," I have deliberately avoided an analysis primarily in terms of the historical development of western civilization, feeling that a freer, more universal, catholic interpretation would do more justice to the varied dimensions and suggestions of these sonnets. For though they do present, without a doubt, a survey of the cultural development of the West, they also delineate human experiences not limited to one caste or one era, experiences with which we are all familiar as individuals. I trust that the overall evolutionary and historical drift of the sequence has been clear, in any case.

Revision of sonnet XI is extensive and of particular interest as it involves sound, meter, imagery, tone, and meaning. The first change one encounters, however, is apparently minor, comprising the elimination of a thoroughly superfluous definite article in the first line: "let the song mount" becomes "let song mount." This familiar treatment of the rejected article is the first of a relatively conservative four such prunings that occur in this poem. It is the instance most worthy of notice, for the omission of the definite article seems to release the line of a burden, and "song," free in its generic expansiveness, now rises, lightly and gaily on the rhythm's flow, in happy consonance with the image itself. The power is generated by the cluster of three monosyllabic words of equal importance and weight, the three stresses scanning as a spondee followed by a trochee. The joyous movement of "again and again," which follows, is more noticeable in the revised line because the three consecutive stresses draw and focus one's attention, while the slight pause that comes naturally after "mount" builds a pressure of anticipation.

Line three of the first quatrain is substantially revised. "For the vegetable patience, the animal grace" becomes "For vegetal patience, for animal courage and grace." The elimination of two definite articles is accomplished without effort or loss. The two syllables salvaged are badly needed, for even with this extra working space, the revised and lengthened line of fourteen syllables proves the longest in the poem. However, in spite of this syllabic abundance, the line reveals an unexceptional five feet, its original four anapests now preceded by an iamb. "Vegetable," a noun which can serve as an adjective, is replaced by the exclusively adjectival "vegetal" which, freed from the burden of an unneeded definite article, gives speedy entry into the flow of the basically anapestic line. This revision seems worthwhile, whether looked at in terms of rhythm or sound. If "vegetable" is pronounced with four syllables, the reading becomes choppy and scansion troubling, with an initial anapest followed by a pyrrhic and an iamb. However (as is more likely particularly for the modern American reader) if "vegetable" is read as three syllables, metrical demands are nicely met, the line consisting of four anapestic feet, but then we must be content with the unpleasant and inappropriate slurring sound of *vejta* or *vetchta*. "Vegetal," on the other hand, is pleasantly precise both in sound and in function. "Animal grace" is retained though with equally laudable "courage" snugly interpolated: "animal courage and grace." The line becomes longer, fuller, but does not in any way suffer a loss of graceful flow.

Revision of the fourth line of the opening quatrain achieves a great improvement in rhythm: "Some people have been happy; there have been great men" becomes "Some have been happy; some, even, were great men." The earlier version reads as disconcerting prose. Its irregular meter, difficult to scan at best, comes as an abrupt interruption to the flow of basically anapestic feet that precede it. As the end-stopped last line of the first stanza, the terminating line to the first movement or idea, and, technically speaking, the end of the first sentence, it should have a rhythm that leads naturally to a firm and solid conclusion at the end of the line. Instead, a baffling array, difficult to decipher, of trochee, iamb, and anapest precedes the final, strangely ineffective spondee. Reasonable scansion is possible only if one accents heavily the initial "Some" and the word "have" both times it appears as if arguing against someone who said, "Life is misery, mankind is an utter failure": "**Some** people **have** been **happy**; there **have** been **great men**." This scansion, presuming a truncation of the final syllable of a trochaic foot at the end of the line, consists of trochee, iamb, iamb, anapest, iamb, truncated trochee. In order to end with a spondee, one could assume two successive amphibrachs preceding it, but this seems somewhat irregular. In any case, however scanned, the line resists a poetic reading, taking on the contours of weakish polemic prose. Revised, the line is still difficult to scan, but it moves forward in two wave-like motions separated by a tension-building group of pauses: "**Some** have been **happy**; **some**, **even**, were **great men**." The rhythmically disturbing "people" is dropped, and the accents fall clearly and naturally on "some" and "happy." After a caesura at the semicolon, the line moves from an accented "some" to an accented "even" with a definite pause between the two. After "even," there is another pause before moving on to the final two accented syllables, "great men." The interruption in the second half of the line, caused by the interjection of "even," gathers the force of the line in an anticipatory suspension that is then followed by the down rush to the final accented syllables, giving the line a natural movement in consonance with its sense that the earlier version lacked.

It is interesting to compare the revision of the line just analyzed with that of the strikingly similar passage concluding "Dover, 1937." In the latter, " . . . Some are temporary heroes: / Some of these people are happy" becomes " . . . Some may be heroes: / Not all of us are unhappy." In both cases, the formulation involving "Some people" being "happy" has been changed, the alteration clearly more radical in "Dover, 1937."

In the first line of the second quatrain, with its open borrowing from Hopkins' "Spring and Fall: To Margaret," a comma in "weeping, and know why" is dropped. Reminiscent of the revision in sonnet VI converting "The rivers flooded or the Empire fell" to "A river flooded or a fortress fell" is the alteration, in the next line, of "Cities and men have fallen" to "Ramparts and souls have fallen." The contrast between the external, material construct and the essentially human is heightened by the specific and concrete nature of the military term used in the revised line. The switch to a double use of synecdoche achieves a sharpness of contrast that the conventional and unevocative "cities and men" could not, so that now the essential difference between the two is graphically clear. The revised line gains depth through the new implication that not only have men died in the body, but souls have been lost as well, an implication that expands the meaning of "fallen," reminds the reader of the tale of Genesis with which this sonnet sequence begins and emphasizes the gulf between the external or material and the internal or spiritual. Revision sharpens the ironic effect of the syllepsis, and a poignancy is achieved that is absent in the earlier version. At the end of this same line, the capitalization is dropped from "the will of the Unjust."

The third line of this stanza must be read in conjunction with the phrase at the end of the preceding line: " . . . the will of the Unjust / Has never lost its power." This is revised to read, " . . . the will of the unjust / Has never lacked an engine." An alliterating *p* for the "princes" that follow is lost, but the conversion of an ordinary expression, lacking in imaginative appeal, to a chillingly suggestive formulation utilizing figuratively a term whose literal meaning carries connotations of mechanized coldness, cruelty, and torture, more than compensates for this loss. The overtones of the word "engine" stimulate the reader through sensual associations as the abstract term "power" cannot.

The last line of the second quatrain undergoes a reduction of all capitals to lower case, following a policy already amply documented. This revision is, of course, in consonance with the reduction in line six of "Unjust" to lower case.

The first tercet has undergone the most extensive, interesting, and successful revisions in the poem. The two versions, in their entirety, follow:

> History opposes its grief to our buoyant song:
> The Good Place has not been; our star has warmed to birth
> A race of promise that has never proved its worth;

Becomes:

> History opposes its grief to our buoyant song,
> To our hope its warning. One star has warmed to birth
> One puzzled species that has yet to prove its worth:

In line with his efforts, already noted in the previous stanza, to eliminate some of the more arbitrary manifestations of his younger, capitalizing days, Auden discards his once beloved "Good Place" (though he retains it intact, as we have seen, in "Whither?"). The entire clause is dropped in favor of a kind of inverted appositive phrase, a quietly cautionary, if purely conceptual formulation, echoing with its abstract antithesis of "hope" and "warning" the partially metaphoric antithesis of "grief" and "buoyant song" in the preceding line. The reversal of direct object and prepositional phrase in the appositional phrase brings about, in conjunction with the preceding line, a kind of chiasmatic effect that is particularly pleasing to the ear.

The change of "our star" to "one star" must be considered together with the substantial revision of the following line. The somewhat unexpected presence of the lonely numerical at the head of the new sentence followed by its repetition at the head of line eleven, reduces sun and *Homo sapiens* to isolated tiny phenomena in an immense and lifeless universe. Looked at from such a perspective, man is seen as at the far end of an inverted telescope, alone and infinitely small, weak and in need of pity, indeed "One puzzled species that has yet to prove its worth." This somewhat pathetic image, replacing the accusatory "race of promise that has never proved its worth," quite transforms the emotional effect of the line. The adjective "puzzled" implies that the species would like to do what it is supposed to, would like to fulfill its promise and prove its worth, but doesn't really know how to go about it. The adverb "yet," which replaces "never," is even more instrumental in changing the tone and direction of the line than is the modifier "puzzled." Now the image is one of a species that may still come out all right, "yet" keeping the door of the future open and nurturing our hope where frigid "never" had frozen it. On the technical level the line retains the alliteration of *p*'s as "promise" is replaced by "puzzled" aided by "species."

One of the most interesting discrepancies between the revisions appearing in *CSP* and those in *Opere Poetiche* occurs in the line just discussed. The version in *Opere Poetiche*, "One puzzled species that has never proved its worth," lies halfway between the severity of the original line and the compassion of the final version. "A race of promise" has already given way to the more sympathetic "One puzzled species," but the inexorable "never proved" has not been replaced by the more hopeful "yet to prove." Here we see the revising poet caught in midstep.

In the first line of the last stanza a semicolon after "false" is reduced to a comma and a comma after "prodigious" is dropped. In the next line, "This passive flower-like people" becomes "the flower-like Hundred Families." Apparently Auden feels that the "passive" is redundant together with "flower-like" and prefers to balance the specific numerical reference to the Chinese Provinces in the last line with an equally specific numerical reference here to the fabled ancestral source of the Chinese people. The alliterating *p*'s of "passive-people" are replaced by the *f*'s and *l*'s of "flower-like Families." In the last line of the poem the metrics are considerably improved by the change from "constructed the earth" to "modified the earth." The first half of the line, consisting of an anapest and two iambs, is followed, after the caesura of the revised version, by three successive iambs to the end of the poem. This pleasing termination replaces an awkward pair of anapestic feet that lent no sense of finality to the poem's conclusion. Metrics aside, the revised version seems more sensible, for though man can and does modify the earth, he does not, strictly speaking, construct it.

XIV (*Journey to a War*)

Yes, we are going to suffer, now; the sky
Throbs like a feverish forehead; pain is real;
The groping searchlights suddenly reveal
The little natures that will make us cry,

Who never quite believed they could exist,
Not where we were. They take us by surprise
Like ugly long-forgotten memories,
And like a conscience all the guns resist.

Behind each sociable home-loving eye
The private massacres are taking place;
All women, Jews, the Rich, the Human Race.

The mountains cannot judge us when we lie:
We dwell upon the earth; the earth obeys
The intelligent and evil till they die. (Auden, *Journey to a War*)

XV (*Journey to a War*)

Engines bear them through the sky: they're free
And isolated like the very rich;
Remote like savants, they can only see
The breathing city as a target which

Requires their skill; will never see how flying
Is the creation of ideas they hate,
Nor how their own machines are always trying
To push through into life. They chose a fate

The islands where they live did not compel.
Though earth may teach our proper discipline,
At any time it will be possible

To turn away from freedom and become,
Bound like the heiress in her mother's womb,
And helpless as the poor have always been. (Auden, *Journey to a War*)

Sonnets XIV and XV from "In Time of War" have been dropped from the sequence. They both deal with Japanese air-raids in China, and what they offer in specificity and immediacy they lack in universality and breadth of suggestion. The problems of the human condition, with which the sonnet sequence continually grapples, are, in these poems, formulated with perhaps too much assurance. Two passages in sonnet XIV that I assume may have particularly displeased Auden are the facile simile "And like a conscience all the guns resist" and the rhetorically effective but not quite honest "the earth obeys / The intelligent and evil till they die." On the other hand, it seems a great pity to lose, with sonnet XV, the memorable images "they can only see / The breathing city as a target," and "Bound like the heiress in her mother's womb."

XVI (*Journey to a War*)

Here war is simple like a monument:
A telephone is speaking to a man;
Flags on a map assert that troops were sent;
A boy brings milk in bowls. There is a plan

For living men in terror of their lives,
Who thirst at nine who were to thirst at noon,
And can be lost and are, and miss their wives,
And, unlike an idea, can die too soon.

But ideas can be true although men die,
And we can watch a thousand faces
Made active by one lie:

And maps can really point to places
Where life is evil now:
Nanking; Dachau. (Auden, *Journey to a War* 253)

XII (*CSP*)

Here war is harmless like a monument:
A telephone is talking to a man;
Flags on a map declare that troops were sent;
A boy brings milk in bowls. There is a plan

For living men in terror of their lives,
Who thirst at nine who were to thirst at noon,
Who can be lost and are, who miss their wives
And, unlike an idea, can die too soon.

Yet ideas can be true, although men die:
For we have seen a myriad faces
Ecstatic from one lie,

And maps can really point to places
Where life is evil now.
Nanking. Dachau. (Auden, *CSP* 133)

Sonnet XII (formerly XVI) has a rhyme scheme of ABAB CDCD EFE FGG. The first rhyme pair in the poem provides an instance of light rhyme, the final rhyming syllable of the first word not receiving a major stress: "monument-sent." The final rhyme pair of the poem provides another example of the use of light rhyme: "now-Dachau." All the other end words are perfect masculine rhymes except for the feminine pair in lines ten and twelve, "faces-places." The meter is iambic pentameter, appearing in the quatrains in the most regular fashion. However, the tercets are less conventional, revealing a syllabic count of ten, nine, six, and nine, six, four in which the only rhyming pair with equal lines is that of lines ten and twelve, each containing nine syllables and four feet. The unusual diminution of feet in the sestet is not arbitrary but serves the definite purpose of funneling and concentrating attention upon the final icily terse line.

Sonnet XII describes the artificiality of war when it is experienced from a safe distance, pays homage to the suffering of the actual soldiers, then turns to the evil of the false ideas that are war's source. The first quatrain describes a scene safe behind the lines, far from the front, where "war is harmless like a monument," a scene of telephones, flags on a map, bowls of milk brought by servants, and plans for battle that will lose others their lives. The second quatrain moves from those plans to the men actually fighting the war "in terror of their lives," and, with a certain professional detachment, conscientiously paints their human vulnerability, making a pointed contrast to the protected world of telephones and maps, and, most of all, ideas, that world in which the war is dealt with through symbols, words, and theories. The first tercet picks up the question of ideas, declaring, "Yet ideas can be true, although men die," reminding us that there are good as well as evil ideas and that to recognize the difference between them is essential, for, as the last stanza points out, it is at least partly because of evil ideas that "maps can really point to places / Where life is evil now."

Revisions in this sonnet are not extensive. In the first quatrain, one word is changed in each of the first three lines. In line one, "Here war is simple" becomes "Here war is harmless." The line gains the alliteration of *h*'s and a new accuracy as well. The opening word signals an implied comparison between conditions "Here" and at the front. However war at the front is not really characterized by complexity but by danger. The foot soldier's war is simple, simpler than that of the general's in a world of telephones and maps. He obeys orders and dies. It is the presence of danger and death at the front that differentiates it from the general's quarters far to the rear and the proud monument far in the future. The revised line makes better sense, to put it simply, than does the original. In line two, "A telephone is speaking to a man" becomes "A telephone is talking to a man." The revision adds an alliterating *t* to the line. In the third line "Flags on a map assert" becomes "Flags on a map declare." The new verb is somewhat stronger in sound and tone and more strictly accurate, since it can mean simply *to manifest*, *to show*, while *assert* always implies a positive statement either in anticipation or in the face of denial or objection. Auden may also have been attracted to *declare* by its root meaning, which, in the present context, would intimate with subtle irony what he has dropped from the opening line, that all seems simple here, *made clear*.

In the second quatrain only line three is touched by revision. Containing an awkward three conjunctive "and's," it loses two of them in favor of a repetitive "who." "And can be lost and are, and miss their wives" becomes "Who can be lost and are, who miss their wives." The change not only eliminates a couple of excessive "and's," but it achieves, in conjunction with the repeated "who" of the preceding line, a buildup of dramatic pressure, even of fear, surpassing that created by the repeated conjunctions.

The most extensive changes in the poem occur in the third stanza. In the first line, only the initial "But" is changed to "Yet," providing the more usual correlative conjunction to go with "although." The next line is substantially rephrased, "And we can watch a thousand faces" becoming "For we have seen a myriad faces." An initial "and" is dropped for the second time in this poem. The evidence of this tercet is made more compelling by the change in tense, "For we have seen" being a declaration of fact, already ascertained and fixed in the safety of the past, while "And we can watch" remains, though a statement, something so far not established, something taken on faith. The frightening quality of the image, already bolstered by the assurance of the past tense, is meant to be further reinforced by the hyperbolic "myriad" replacing the unexcitingly conservative "thousand." I am not certain I prefer the new modifier to its simpler, if too modest, Germanic predecessor. The participial phrase completing the image is changed from "Made active by one lie" to an adjectival phrase without verbal, "Ecstatic from one lie." The violent modifier, with its explosive *k*'s and *t*'s, succeeds by its very sound as well as by its associations in calling forth the frenzied faces of desperate believers, where the combination of an unnecessary past participle of an abstract verb with a relatively tame adjective does not. The revision of these two lines results in a graphic image that speaks to both intellect and senses, and, accordingly, to the emotions as well.

In the last stanza the colon ending the penultimate line is changed to a period as is the semicolon separating the two words of the last line. These seemingly minor punctuation changes are most effective in intensifying the tight-lipped, concentrated, frigid concision of the poem's last line, four sharp syllables surrounded by silence, cold as steel clicking shut. The diminution of each successive line in the last stanza leads the reader, visually and rhythmically, to the focal point and terminus of the poem, performing the function that the twelfth line itself assigns to maps. In a silence created by the loss of several expected feet and the presence of three periods enclosing from all sides the two disyllabic place names, the poem ends with the slamming of iron doors: "Nanking. Dachau."

XVIII (*Journey to a War*)

Far from the heart of culture he was used:
Abandoned by his general and his lice,
Under a padded quilt he closed his eyes
And vanished. He will not be introduced

When this campaign is tidied into books:
No vital knowledge perished in his skull;
His jokes were stale; like wartime, he was dull;
His name is lost for ever like his looks.

He neither knew nor chose the Good, but taught us,
And added meaning like a comma, when
He turned to dust in China that our daughters

Be fit to love the earth, and not again
Disgraced before the dogs; that, where are waters,
Mountains and houses, may be also men. (Auden, *Journey to a
War* 254)

XIII (CSP)

Far from a cultural centre he was used:
Abandoned by his general and his lice,
Under a padded quilt he turned to ice
And vanished. He will never be perused

When this campaign is tidied into books:
No vital knowledge perished in that skull;
His jokes were stale; like wartime, he was dull;
His name is lost for ever like his looks.

Though runeless, to instructions from headquarters
He added meaning like a comma when
He joined the dust of China, that our daughters

Might keep their upright carriage, not again
Be shamed before the dogs, that, where are waters,
Mountains and houses, may be also men. (Auden, *CSP* 134)

Journey to a War's sonnets XVII and XVIII are companion pieces dealing with the common soldier. They appear in reverse order in *CSP* (sonnets XIV and XIII) though the change in position does not seem of great importance.

Sonnet XIII (formerly XVIII) has a rhyme scheme of ABBA CDDC EFE FEF. The only feminine rhymes are in lines nine, eleven, and thirteen. In the earlier version a number of off-rhymes are replaced either by a perfect or almost perfect rhyme. In the first stanza both rhymes in the original are approximate, more than assonance, less than full rhyme: "lice-eyes" and "used-introduced." Both off-rhymes are converted to full rhymes, "eyes" giving way to "ice" and "introduced" to "perused." This type of revision, as we have seen has already appeared in "The Sphinx." In the sestet, "taught us," an off-rhyme for "daughters" and "waters," is replaced by "headquarters," still not a perfect rhyme because of the presence of the weakly pronounced first *r*, but closer than its predecessor. The poem is in perfect iambic pentameter if one scans "general" in line two as disyllabic.

This poem turns to the nameless soldier at the front who dies "Abandoned by his general and his lice." He is described largely in negative terms, the permanence of his facelessness and namelessness being assured. After the octave's depressing picture, the sestet seems to rise up rather polemically to proclaim that this unknown dead illiterate "added meaning like a comma when / He joined the dust of China, that our daughters / Might keep their upright carriage" and "that, where are waters, / Mountains and houses, may be also men."

The beauty of the last line and a half sits strangely next to the politician's jargon that precedes it. It is difficult to decide whether Auden means the last five lines as a serious panegyric or not. The most satisfactory interpretation involves the assumption that "our daughters . . . their upright carriage . . . shamed before the dogs" is intended as a bitter mimicry of the platitudinous insincerities of the officialdom's speeches, while the last line and a half represent Auden's true epitaph for the common soldier. John Fuller evidently accepts the sestet as a sincere, if propagandistic, paean, saying of the sonnet that it "pays rather obvious respects to the fate of the common man in war," and of the passage concerning "our daughters," that it "smacks a little of questions about rape at a tribunal . . . " (Fuller, *Reader's Guide* 127). My less literal reading, I believe, does the poem more justice.

The revisions in sonnet XIII are fairly substantial. Those of quatrain one are particularly effective. In the first line, "the heart of culture" becomes "a cultural centre." The definite article gives way to the indefinite, while a punningly metaphoric landscape retires in favor of actual, if generalized, geography. Perhaps because he employs *paysage moralise* so frequently, Auden felt that in this particular case, when an extensive metaphoric reading was not called for and would, in fact, involve his "heart of culture" in a most heavy-handed sort of humor, he had better make it clear that his intentions were simpler and more direct. The pun is dropped, but irony is maintained by the use of a term eminently appropriate to a tourist guide and ludicrously alien to a world of war.

The fine revision of line three should be looked at not only in terms of its own frighteningly enriched imagery but in terms of its relationship to the preceding line, which, itself, undergoes no alteration:

> Abandoned by his general and his lice,
> Under a padded quilt he closed his eyes

Becomes:

> Abandoned by his general and his lice,
> Under a padded quilt he turned to ice.

This revision involves the conversion of a nicely understated though rather ordinary image to a fruitfully shocking one. That a man should close his eyes under a padded quilt is most usual, that he should then "vanish," as the following line immediately informs us, is rather a jolt, though only for an instant, since we quickly recognize that this is in fact the soldier's expected death. We know that this abandoned soldier is dying, so the emotional effect of the description depends entirely upon the technique of the poet, not at all upon the discovery of the mere fact. In line three, the original version gives us a quiet image that implies rest and perhaps even comfort, relying upon the sudden verb of the following line to make the soldier's death vivid. In the revised version, line three itself provides us with a shock, presenting us with a padded quilt associated with softness and warmth, then showing us beneath it a man "turned to ice." Not only does the image of ice juxtapose chillingly with the padded quilt, but it represents one step or stage in the irrevocable progression of a horrid metaphoric metamorphosis in which human flesh, once useful to generals and lice, therefore unquestionably living, turns to lifeless ice, thence to nothing. The shock of the final verb, "vanish," is given an added force by the revision of line three, since the introduction of the image of ice makes the man's dying reminiscent of the changes of state observed in chemistry lab, in which a solid becomes a liquid, and the liquid then "vanishes" as a vapor before our eyes. The revised image of line three, with the painful irony of its seeming paradox, gives a kind of sardonic echo to the horrible humor of the preceding line's syllepsis, "Abandoned by his general and his lice." This extensive analysis should make it clear that the revision of line three, which John Whitehead considers an unhappy example of the "correction of imperfect rhymes" ("Vin Audenaire" 492), in fact serves most effectively to add an almost surrealistic force to the imagery of the stanza.

No sooner is the soldier dead than we are told, "He will not be introduced / When this campaign is tidied into books." The main clause, comprising the second half of line four, is revised to read, "He will never be perused." The intentionally inappropriate jaunty irony not only remains but is somewhat strengthened by the use of a term which might apply well enough to a literal as well as a literary encounter. The very absurdity of the idea gives the image an added ironic force. Of course, we see here again the conversion of an imperfect rhyme matching a voiced with an unvoiced *s* to a perfect rhyme.

The only revision of the second stanza is the change from "his skull" to "that skull." The change makes the line more brutal and scornful, emphasizing the soldier's lowly position. There is a tone of disparaging irony, even humor, that was absent in the earlier version. This grim irony is a continuation of the tone set in the first stanza. Of course the indictment will be against us, the general, the confident stay-at-homes, the safe readers and writers, should we accept at face value the apparent mockery of the dead. The mockery is of us, with our books about campaigns and our cultural centers, our vital knowledge and our lively jokes, our fundamental belief in our superiority. This revision also eliminates a too rapid repetition of the personal pronoun, appearing, as it does, at the head of the next line.

The sestet undergoes more extensive revision than does the octave. The first line of the first tercet is completely rewritten. "He neither knew nor chose the Good, but taught us" becomes "Though runeless, to instructions from headquarters." No longer presuming to judge a peasant's knowledge of the Good, and happy enough to escape the Platonic formulation itself, Auden shifts to the mundane and gives us an illiterate peasant who, though letters are meaningless symbols to him, is, by his own life and death, a meaningful symbol to us, small but essential, "like a comma." He obeyed "instructions from headquarters" which he himself could neither read nor understand and, with his death, gave those instructions a meaning they had lacked. The simile of the comma remains somewhat vague in the earlier version, suggestive but far from indicative, but in the revised version the grammatical connection between lines nine and ten unites it with the new image of "instructions from headquarters," giving to the soldier a full figurative existence as the comma that makes sense out of gibberish. His role as essential comma counterbalances the fact that "He will never be perused / When this campaign is tidied into books." The revision of line nine, then, eliminates a Platonic abstraction, gives the image of the following line a complete figurative framework, and transforms the two lines together into an appropriately literary figurative response to the soldier's empty literary future so ironically delineated in lines four and five. This extensive revision also replaces the humorous off-rhyme of "taught us" for "daughters" with "headquarters" which, though imperfect, is much closer.

The second line of the first tercet remains basically intact, only an initial "and" being converted to "he," and a comma after the word "comma" dropped. Both of these minor changes are dictated by the extensive revisions in the preceding line which originally consisted of the main clause with a compound predicate but stands revised to an elliptical subordinate clause and a prepositional phrase dependent together upon the main clause with its subject "he" that now constitutes line ten. We have already encountered the same sort of syntactical revision employed to facilitate the elimination of initial "and's" in a number of the earlier sonnets. In this particular case the entire tenth line before the comma was parenthetical, but the revision of the ninth line, making line ten the main clause, obviates the need for the comma.

In the last line of the first tercet, "He turned to dust in China" becomes "He joined the dust of China." The change in verb emphasizes the fact that dust is both the source and end of all men, that, after we leave it for our years of life, it remains patiently awaiting our return. One is reminded, somehow, of the peasant in sonnet IV who, while still living, "took his colour from the earth."

Extensive revision continues into the last stanza. The first line and a half are changed from "Be fit to love the earth, and not again / Disgraced before the dogs" to "Might keep their upright carriage, not again / Be shamed before the dogs." The earlier version seems a false sort of rhetoric, whether intended seriously or as a parody of a politician's speech. Why could not "our daughters" love the earth, even if they have suffered defeat and ravishment? Is not the earth itself ravished by invaders, the dust humble and patient? The revision brings the rhetoric onto a more ordinary plane, speaking now of the outer garments of pride, "upright carriage." It is interesting to note that Auden has chosen to discard the earlier, unironic revision, "human carriage," appearing in *Opere Poetiche*, in favor of this rather hackneyed phrase, so suitable to the lips of any demagogue, when taken in the usual metaphoric manner, while quite in consonance with the grim facts, if taken on the basest literal level. The expression functions successfully on two levels at once, the net effect being an accumulation of rather grotesque humor and a sense of ridicule whose victim can only be the phrase-mongering speechmaker. The revised complete predicate, one syllable longer than its predecessor, handily allows Auden to lop another "and" from the poem. The revision of "Disgraced" to "Be shamed" in the penultimate line sacrifices the alliteration of "Disgraced-dogs," but achieves a more accurate description. "Disgraced" implies societies standards and codes as the norm and society as the judge, whereas shame seems more descriptive of an inner state and a self-condemnation. Though the words are synonyms, shame carries more personal and emotional overtones. Though the word "disgraced" cuts sharply at the fallen one, the words "be shamed" strike a much deeper blow.

XVII (*Journey to a War*)

They are and suffer; that is all they do:
A bandage hides the place where each is living,
His knowledge of the world restricted to
The treatment that the instruments are giving.

And lie apart like epochs from each other
—Truth in their sense is how much they can bear;
It is not talk like ours, but groans they smother—
And are remote as plants; we stand elsewhere.

For who when healthy can become a foot?
Even a scratch we can't recall when cured,
But are boist'rous in a moment and believe

In the common world of the uninjured, and cannot
Imagine isolation. Only happiness is shared,
And anger, and the idea of love. (Auden, *Journey to a War* 254)

XVI (*CSP*)

They are and suffer; that is all they do:
A bandage hides the place where each is living,
His knowledge of the world restricted to
A treatment metal instruments are giving.

They lie apart like epochs from each other
(Truth in their sense is how much they can bear;
It is not talk like ours but groans they smother),
From us remote as plants: we stand elsewhere.

For who when healthy can become a foot?
Even a scratch we can't recall when cured,
But are boisterous in a moment and believe

Reality is never injured, cannot
Imagine isolation: joy can be shared,
And anger, and the idea of love. (Auden, *CSP* 134)

Sonnet XIV (formerly XVII) has a rhyme scheme of ABAB CDCD EFG
EFG. In the first quatrain lines one and three form a perfect masculine rhyme
pair, lines two and four a perfect feminine rhyme pair. In the second quatrain,
the first and third lines end in perfect feminine rhymes, but the second and
fourth end in a light rhyme, "bear-elsewhere." Similar examples of light
rhyme, in which the final rhyming syllable of one of the match words is
unstressed, occur, as we have noticed, as the start and close of sonnet XII.
In the sestet consonance prevails, the rhyming pairs being "foot-cannot,"
"cured-shared," and "believe-love." The octave offers no metrical surprises,
obediently displaying a regular iambic pentameter pattern, with the usual
unaccented eleventh syllable at the end of every line with a feminine ending.
In the first tercet, however, the last line has an unexpected eleventh syllable
in both versions; in the original version the word "boisterous" appears with
an apostrophe to indicate an elision in the middle of the word, keeping the
line from stretching to an even more unorthodox twelve syllables, and, in
the revised version, though the apostrophe is dropped, the line's scansion
requires the same elided reading as before. In the last stanza, revision affects
the length of two lines, the first being diminished from a thirteen syllable,
five foot line containing two anapestic feet to an eleven syllable line of conventional iambic pentameter, the second being reduced from a fourteener, a
line of seven iambic feet, to an eleven syllable line of five feet, ending with
an anapestic foot. This shortening of the two lines brings them into harmony
with the five foot, decasyllabic line that is characteristic of this and most of
the other sonnets in the sequence.

This poem also deals with the common soldier, not, this time, the one who
"Under a padded quilt turned to ice," but those who manage to survive, at
least for a time, and lie in the hospital, heavily swathed and separated from
the rest of the world by their bandages and their pain. The octave describes
them in their isolated misery: "They are and suffer; that is all they do" and
"Truth in their sense is how much they can bear." Their distance from each
other and, even more, from us, the healthy, is a central image: "They lie
apart like epochs from each other," "From us remote as plants: we stand
elsewhere." The sestet turns to the inability of the healthy to comprehend the
insular existence of the suffering, their complete concentration upon their illness or injury: "For who when healthy can become a foot?" The healthy "cannot / Imagine isolation," since their inner experience is so different from that
of the sick and wounded. As Auden somberly concludes, only "Joy can be

shared, / And anger, and the idea of love." Focusing upon the wounded in the octave and the uncomprehending healthy in the sestet, this sonnet effectively depicts the loneliness of the injured sufferer and the gulf that lies between him and all other men.

There is comparatively limited revision in sonnet XIV, most of it restricted to the final stanza. In the first stanza, only the last line is touched by revision, "The treatment that the instruments are giving" becoming "A treatment metal instruments are giving." The initial definite article is reduced to an indefinite article, and an optional relative pronoun and definite article are replaced by a well-chosen adjective that dramatically evokes the helpless, frightening, lonely state of these wounded whose only contact with the outside world is the cold inhuman touch of "metal instruments." Revision of this line eliminates two of the four definite articles that are dropped in this poem.

In the second stanza, the initial "and" is dropped in favor of a clarifying pronoun. Though the poem begins with the subject "They," by the end of the second line it has become the singular "each." The plural conjugation of the verb that appears immediately in the second stanza is somewhat confusing without a proximate subject since the previous two lines had focused upon a single soldier. In the following two lines the dashes are replaced by parentheses as were the dashes in the first line of sonnet VII. In the last line, the foggy Rilkean "And are remote as plants" becomes "From us remote as plants." For the second time in the stanza, an initial "and" is dropped. More important, the isolation of the patients is now definitely seen against the foil of the healthy, not merely as a fact of their own condition but as a reflection upon all of us. They are, of course, "remote as plants" from each other as well as from us, as the first line of this stanza makes clear, but by prefixing to the quietly startling image the prepositional phrase, "From us," Auden calls attention to the gulf that separates each of us from these other human beings, a gulf that we, apparently, are powerless to bridge. The explanatory phrase at the head of the line also prepares one for the line's final word, "we stand elsewhere." Bringing us, the healthy, into the poem, emphasizes the unhappy otherness of the patients, while seeming to suggest, at the same time, that it is we, the healthy poet and readers, free from dominating pain, who are aware of their remoteness, not they who merely experience it.

Except for the elimination of that unnecessary apostrophe signifying elision in the word "boisterous," the first tercet remains unchanged. The second, however, is extensively revised:

> In the common world of the uninjured, and cannot
> Imagine isolation. Only happiness is shared,
> And anger, and the idea of love.

Becomes:

> Reality is never injured, cannot
> Imagine isolation: joy can be shared,
> And anger, and the idea of love.

The revised first line, reduced from thirteen to eleven syllables, is not only more succinct but has gained a fertile ambiguousness. Is reality, for the healthy, in fact, a world without injuries, or is it their own vision of life which refuses to be injured by nightmarish unreal things that happen to others such as mutilation, pain, suffering, and death? However one reads it, the suggestiveness of the revised line enriches the poem. Turning to technical concerns, the longer original line is most difficult to scan. Unless one is willing to give the stress in the final word to the second syllable, against the usual pronunciation which accents the first, one ends up with three iambs sandwiched between an initial an terminal anapest, with an unwelcome hypercatalectic syllable at the end. However, if one does shift the accent in "cannot" to the second syllable, the line becomes, after the initial anapest, a succession of five iambs. In any case, no wrenchings of stress are necessary for a smooth scansion of the revised line: it is in regular iambic pentameter. This line, then, is cut to half the words of the original version, fits the basic iambic pentameter pattern of the other lines, and gains, in its succinct formulation, a suggestiveness that the longer line lacks.

The rephrasing of the penultimate line is designed to suggest even more emphatically the distance between the insular wounded and the rest of us. The explanatory "Only happiness is shared" is dropped, and a succinct statement of fact replaces it: "Joy can be shared." This declaration, thanks to the unadorned manner of its presentation, conveys an acute sense of the incontrovertible nature of life's facts. Its unemotional formulation, imitative of life's utter indifference to our sufferings and desires, manages to evoke a reactive pity in the reader who, after all, wants to be human and feel. The pity is both for those who "lie apart . . . remote as plants" and for the healthy as well, walled in from the world of the ill, unable ultimately to understand and share the others' misery, unable to be compassionate as, ideally, they think men should be. Even in tone, the stark statement teaches a necessary lesson about the nature of reality, a lesson showing us that as the wounded "lie apart," so too are the healthy bound by limits and barriers they cannot transverse. The line achieves a tone of sad but collected acceptance of necessity.

XIX (*Journey to a War*)

But in the evening the oppression lifted;
The peaks came into focus; it had rained.
Across the lawns and cultured flowers
Drifted the conversation of the highly trained.

The gardeners watched them pass and priced their shoes;
A chauffeur waited, reading in the drive,
For them to finish their exchange of views;
It seemed a picture of the private life.

Far off, no matter what good they intended,
The armies waited for a verbal error
With all the instruments for causing pain:

And on the issue of their charm depended
A land laid waste, with all its young men slain,
The women weeping, and the towns in terror. (Auden, *Journey to a War* 255)

XV (*CSP*)

As evening fell the day's oppression lifted;
Tall peaks came into focus; it had rained:
Across wide lawns and cultured flowers drifted
The conversation of the highly trained.

Thin gardeners watched them pass and priced their shoes;
A chauffeur waited, reading in the drive,
For them to finish their exchange of views:
It looked a picture of the way to live.

Far off, no matter what good they intended,
Two armies waited for a verbal error
With well-made implements for causing pain,

And on the issue of their charm depended
A land laid waste with all its young men slain,
Its women weeping, and its towns in terror. (Auden, *CSP* 135)

Sonnet XV (formerly XIX) has a rhyme scheme of ABAB CDCD EFD EGF. Only one rhyme is imperfect. Lines six and eight end, in the earlier version, with "drive" and "life," a case of assonance in which the final consonants are proximate, being the voiced and unvoiced forms of the same fricative. This matching of related fricatives or spirants is similar to the matching of voiced and unvoiced *s*'s noted in the original versions of "The Sphinx" and sonnet XIII. Revision changes this rhyme pair to "drive" and "live," the verbal infinitive providing a consonance and an eye rhyme in place of the assonance of its noun and predecessor. The poem is in iambic pentameter, and there are no metrically aberrant lines.

The sonnet begins by depicting the calm, ordered, and elegant world of high level officials, if not the leaders of nations, a world of "lawns and cultured flowers," served by gardeners and chauffeurs, so perfect "It looked a picture of the way to live." The octave's charming still-life portrayal of civilized refinement is followed by the sestet's corrective rejoinder in which we are reminded that the armies, "far off," are merely waiting "for a verbal error / With well-made implements for causing pain," and that, no matter how cultivated the leaders, "on the issue of their charm depended / A land laid waste with all its young men slain." The antithesis between the world of the actual combatant and the world of those who pull the strings or just watch, already set forth in sonnets XII, XIII, and XIV, finds perhaps too explicit expression in this poem.

Revision of sonnet XV is moderate, but it does provide excellent examples of the way in which definite articles can be effectively replaced by a variety of modifiers. Eight definite articles are replaced in the course of the poem, three of them in the first stanza.

The first line of the poem is completely recast. "But in the evening the oppression lifted" becomes "As evening fell the day's oppression lifted." The revised line, though it is identical in length with the line as it originally stood, manages to introduce a double set of antitheses that are woven together in a pleasing and witty manner. "Evening" is set off against "day," while "fell" is set off against "lifted." The amusement of this line comes from the fact that the two verbs, functioning figuratively, run counter to each other and seemingly contradict. When we speak of evening falling, we have in mind the curtain of a theater falling over the stage, blacking it out. Evening falls and ends the day by covering it in darkness. However, in this particular case, the falling of evening is accompanied by the lifting of "the day's oppression," and, instead of a stage concealed and a play ended, we are shown a scene newly revealed, a stage set, with actors, principal and secondary, in clear view. A definite article is dropped, making way for the verb "fell" which, quite appropriately, provides a kind of inverted consonance or double alliteration for "lifted."

The next two lines each drops a definite article in favor of a descriptive adjective. "The peaks" become "Tall peaks," while "the lawns" become "wide lawns." This interpolation of descriptive detail accentuates the feeling of a stage set being described, with background looming high but distant behind the spacious foreground.

In the second quatrain, "The gardeners" become "Thin gardeners," and we not only see them better, but understand, without even thinking, why they price the shoes of the elegant leaders strolling by. The last line of this stanza undergoes significant revision. "It seemed a picture of the private life" becomes "It looked a picture of the way to live." The alliterating *p*'s of "picture" and "private" are lost, but the alliterating *l*'s of "looked" and "live" are gained. The meaning of the line has been clarified. "A picture of the private life" remains rather obscure to me, but "a picture of the way to live" is clear enough, and the fact that gardener, chauffeur, and even poet and reader could be tempted by such a picture seems quite understandable. Of course this line is highly ironic since we know that this charming evening get-together, "no matter what good they intended," must result, "far off," not in changes of lifestyle, but in "young men slain" and "women weeping."

In the third stanza both revisions involve the substitution of an adjective for the definite article. The change in the second line from "The armies" to "Two armies" is not of major consequence, but the revision in the third line of "all the instruments" to "well-made implements" is well worth examining. *All*, a non-specific adjective of numerical totality frequently employed by Auden in *Journey to a War* (and often cut in revision), is dropped, together with an unneeded definite article, in favor of the coldly impersonal, scientifically objective modifier "well-made." At the same time, "instruments," already unpleasant enough in its present context, is transformed to the even more discomforting "implements." Instruments are articles of equipment or tools, but implements are specifically instruments "essential to the performance or execution of something," according to *Webster's Collegiate Dictionary*. By the very nature of the noun used, our attention is instantly cast forward and focused upon that "something," in this case "causing pain." Of course, using "well-made," a perfectly objective descriptive term, in this context, throws an even more ghoulish light on the entire affair. The term itself, we might note, fits neatly in its place, providing convenient consonantal links in both directions, echoing the *w* of "with" on one side and the *m*'s of "implements" on the other. As for "implements" itself, that word not only points to "pain" by the nuance of its meaning but also links to it, undemonstratively, through its *p* sound.

The expression "all the instruments" appeared again, within a year of *Journey to a War*'s publication, in the original version of Auden's famous "In Memory of W.B. Yeats": "O all the instruments agree / The day of his death was a dark cold day." It is interesting to note that, just as almost identical formulations in sonnet XI and "Dover, 1937" are similarly eliminated by revision, the expression "all the instruments" has disappeared from both the Yeats elegy and sonnet XV in *CSP*. In the case of the sonnet, as we have seen, it is replaced by "well-made implements." In the revised version of the Yeats elegy, "O all the instruments agree" is transformed to the limiting "What instruments we have agree." If Auden had dropped the expression from only one of the two poems, we could have assumed he was doing so simply to avoid the embarrassment of self-plagiarism. However, since this is not the case, one must seek other explanations, as I have done above. We will encounter, in the first line of sonnet XIX, an interesting third revision, paralleling in a modest way these two, the locution "all the apparatus" being revised to "all our apparatus."

In the last stanza of sonnet XV two more definite articles are dropped, though in this case the gain is less noticeable than in earlier instances. The last line is changed from "the women weeping, and the towns in terror" to "Its women weeping, and its towns in terror." In this case, it seems to me that the specificity introduced by the revision is not of great significance, since the image was just as clear while the definite articles stood.

XX (*Journey to a War*)

> They carry terror with them like a purse,
> And flinch from the horizon like a gun;
> And all the rivers and the railways run
> Away from Neighbourhood as from a curse.
>
> They cling and huddle in the new disaster
> Like children sent to school, and cry in turn;
> For Space has rules they cannot hope to learn,
> Time speaks a language they will never master.
>
> We live here. We lie in the Present's unopened
> Sorrow; its limits are what we are.
> The prisoner ought never to pardon his cell.
>
> Can future ages ever escape so far,
> Yet feel derived from everything that happened,
> Even from us, that even this was well? (Auden, *Journey to a War*)

Auden has dropped sonnet XX from the sequence, perhaps because it seemed to him, on later reading, that he had been more concerned with rhetorical effect than with accurate imagery and precise distinctions. It is from this poem that Spears takes his two examples when he speaks of Auden's passing "vice of over-facility, of making tricks of style mechanical (as in 'They carry terror with them like a purse, / And flinch from the horizon like a gun') ... ." These similes (there are, in fact, four of them in the poem) resemble in formulation those of rejected sonnet XIV, particularly "And like a conscience all the guns resist."

XXI (*Journey to a War*)

The life of man is never quite completed;
The daring and the chatter will go on:
But, as an artist feels his power gone,
These walk the earth and know themselves defeated.

Some could not bear nor break the young and mourn for
The wounded myths that once made nations good,
Some lost a world they never understood,
Some saw too clearly all that man was born for.

Loss is their shadow-wife, Anxiety
Receives them like a grand hotel; but where
They may regret they must; their life, to hear

The call of the forbidden cities, see
The stranger watch them with a happy stare,
And Freedom hostile in each home and tree (Auden, *Journey to a War* 255).

XVI (*CSP*)

Our global story is not yet completed,
Crime, daring, commerce, chatter will go on,
But, as narrators find their memory gone,
Homeless, disterred, these know themselves defeated.

Some could not like nor change the young and mourn for
Some wounded myth that once made children good,
Some lost a world they never understood,
Some saw too clearly all that man was born for.

Loss is their shadow-wife, Anxiety
Receives them like a grand hotel, but where
They may regret they must: their doom to bear

Love for some far forbidden country, see
A native disapprove them with a stare
And Freedom's back in every door and tree. (Auden, *CSP* 135)

Sonnet XVI (formerly XXI) has a rhyme scheme of ABBA CDDC EFF EFE. The rhymes in the quatrains are all perfect, but in the tercets there is a light rhyme of "Anxiety" with "see" and "tree," and, in the original, a consonance of "hear" with "where" and "stare," which is then revised to the full rhyme "bear." In the quatrains, the enclosing lines end in feminine rhymes and contain an eleventh syllable each, while the enclosed lines end in masculine rhymes and are decasyllabic. In the tercets, all lines are decasyllabic, even line seven with its feminine light rhyme at the end. The poem is, as one might expect, in iambic pentameter.

This sonnet, as Fuller says, "is about the alienation of the imperialist class" (Fuller, *Reader's Guide* 127). The first quatrain begins by assuring the reader that "Crime, daring, commerce, chatter will go on," in spite of the fact that today's exploiters of the less progressive nations and peoples are being dislodged and defeated. The second quatrain briefly analyzes the motives, attitudes, and understanding of the imperialists, finding three types: those who "could not like nor change the young," and, wishing to control them, now "mourn for / Some wounded myth that once made children good"; those who simply exploit the more primitive regions and their inhabitants without any pretense of philosophical justification, in fact without thought, understanding neither the oppressed nor themselves; and, finally, those who, cynically viewing life as a ruthless struggle for domination, decide to play the ugly game for whatever it is worth. The sestet describes them in their defeat, speaking in the first tercet of loss, anxiety, and regret, in the second of their unhappy isolation in the land suddenly revealed as alien and inimical, a colony in revolt, where nothing but hostility and someone else's freedom greet them in the eyes and doorways of the transformed populace. When we are told "Their doom is to bear / Love for some far forbidden country," it seems an ironic echo of man's lingering love for the paradise from which he was originally expelled, the Genesis tale retold in sonnets I and II.

The revisions in this sonnet are quite extensive, most of them occurring in the first and last stanzas. In the first quatrain, every line undergoes considerable revision:

The life of man is never quite completed;
The daring and the chatter will go on:
But, as an artist feels his power gone,
These walk the earth and know themselves defeated.

Becomes:

> Our global story is not yet completed,
> Crime, daring, commerce, chatter will go on,
> But, as narrators find their memory gone,
> Homeless, disterred, these know themselves defeated.

Revision of the first line gives it a new perspective and a new tone unappreciated by John Whitehead who comments briefly in his review: "The journalese of 'Our global story' . . . is not to be preferred to "The life of man'" (Whitehead, "Vin Audenaire" 492). The expression "global story" puts man's life in its proper place, viewing it in terms of the entire universe. This change is accompanied by the seemingly slight shift in adverb from "quite" to "yet." In the original line, though man is viewed ironically, the tone is a rather light and cheerful one, as we are humorously assured that "The life of man is never quite completed." Now the irony has a heavier, grimmer ring to it, for although we are told that our story will still go on, the implication is that it will not go on forever, that it is limited in time just as our world, only a globe, is limited in space. A definite article, the first word of the poem, has been dropped from the revised version. It is the first of four definite articles eliminated from the first stanza alone, and one of eight pared from the sonnet as a whole.

In the second line, two definite articles and one connective "and" are dropped, their places taken by nouns that help fill in the picture of "Our global story." Admirable abstract "daring" is now preceded by one of its less laudable manifestations or results, "Crime." Idle and harmless "chatter" is now preceded by its active, aggressive, and profitable version, "commerce." Now four descriptive nouns provide a rounded portrait of human existence, touching upon the nefarious, the admirable and noble, the active but selfish, and the mildly meaningless and wasteful. The two new substantives add concreteness of imagery to the line, as well as bringing to it the alliteration of their initial consonants.

Just as "Crime" and "commerce" bring to the second line a specificity that the abstract "daring" and generalized "chatter" do not, so, in the third line, revision replaces the general and abstract with the particular. The combination of "artist" and "power" remains too undefined to provide a distinct image. Not only could "artist" suggest a wide range of creative activity, but "power" could apply equally well, in the strength of its abstractness, to a boxer, a builder, a chess player, or a general. "Artist" is replaced by "narrators," an intentionally humble and neutral substitute, for this term in the analogy is matched with "these" defeated imperialists, and the positive overtones of "artist" are clearly inappropriate. The all-inclusive "power" is replaced by "memory," a quality that is specifically essential for the success of the narrator. The tone of the line is changed by the revision. The grave sympathy called forth by the original line gives way to a kind of humorous pathos as the shadowy image of a failing artist is replaced by the rather ridiculous image of a talker forgetting his lines. The word "narrator" evokes no emotional response, whereas "artist" and even storyteller have sympathetic overtones.

In line four, revision eliminates another definite article and a connective "and," making room for the two new modifiers. However, the less compact earlier version evokes in its simple biblical style an emotion that the revised version does not. The homelessness of the disinherited colonialists is communicated better by the simple and stark statement, "These walk the earth," than by the two adjectives, the explicit "Homeless" and the awkward "disterred," which literally proclaim their loss of home and land. Auden may have decided to cut the simpler biblical phrase because, like the previous line's "an artist feels his power gone," it conveyed too much dignity and evoked a strong sympathy that he felt was inappropriate considering the circumstances.

The second quatrain undergoes relatively few changes. In the first line, "Some could not bear nor break the young" is modified to "Some could not like nor change the young." The forceful alliterative verb pair with its violence of sound and meaning gives way to a softer, less dramatic formulation. A certain excitement and intensity are sacrificed in the interest of honesty and accuracy. In general, the colonialist thought little at all about his native "children" busily following his instructions. He might perhaps have admitted to not particularly liking them but would have been most surprised to hear that he "could not bear" them. In the next line, "The wounded myths that once made nations good" becomes "Some wounded myth that once made children good." The conversion of the initial definite article to "some" results in all four lines of this quatrain beginning with the same word, giving to the stanza a kind of incantatory, mythologizing flavor. The effect is rather like that aimed at by the recurrent initial "and's" so prevalent throughout these sonnets in their original form. Of course in the present case the effect is carefully limited to the one stanza; "some" appears only once elsewhere in the sonnet, and then not at the head of a line. In fact, with the pointed exception of the second quatrain, there are no lines in the poem that begin with the same word. The introduction of the indefinite adjective in place of the definite article makes the use of the plural form of "myth" pointless, so it is changed to the singular. The most important change in the line is the conversion of "nations" to "children." Modern nations as we know them have never been good, but we like to think that "our children," whether our own offspring or the child-like races of the backward lands, are good when they behave as we would like them to. The "wounded myth" is any story that once served to keep primitive people properly subservient to the technologically superior invaders, but that no longer does. Of course the term children continues the ironic imagery already suggested by the previous line's figurative locution, "the young." It is worth remarking, before going on, that Auden, as he did in sonnet XI, again draws on Hopkins' "Spring and Fall: To Margaret," borrowing the end rhyme of this quatrain's first and last lines from the conclusion of Hopkins' sonnet: "It is the blight man was born for, / It is Margaret you mourn for."

The first tercet undergoes minor changes of punctuation, a semicolon in the second line becoming a comma, another in the third line becoming a colon. The revision of the last part of the third line is best examined together with the last stanza, as it is linked to it grammatically and cannot be understood without it. This concluding passage of three and a half lines tells of the future in store for the unhappy colonialists, on the brink of failure and obsolescence.

> . . . their life, to hear
>
> The call of the forbidden cities, see
> The stranger watch them with a happy stare,
> And Freedom hostile in each home and tree.

Becomes:

> . . . their doom to bear
>
> Love for some far forbidden country, see
> A native disapprove them with a stare
> And Freedom's back in every door and tree.

In the last line of the third stanza, the consonance of "hear" with "where" and "stare" is replaced by the full rhyme of "bear," a word salvaged from the original version of line five. The verb, with its suggestion of weight and suffering, is nicely matched by the new noun with its mournful sound and gloomy overtones. "Doom," originally a statute, law, or decree, came to mean a judgment, specifically the Last Judgment. Although in its general sense of destiny or fate it could have carried positive connotations, in fact the word has come to mean only unhappy destiny, usually implying failure or death. "Doom" introduces the tone appropriate to the content of the last stanza immediately. This revised language at the end of the third stanza has an additional strength, the ability to evoke the image of our progenitors cast out of Eden, a scene of which the imperialists' fate is a kind of modern parody. This poem's protagonists, like Adam and Eve, are expelled because they have failed to obey a divine commandment, in this case "Love thy neighbor as thyself." Also, like Adam and Eve, they have exploited the advantages of their power, while neglecting its responsibilities. The echoes of the biblical expulsion become inescapable with the revised version of the first line of the last stanza. Adam and Eve, having failed in their stewardship, are doomed "to bear / Love for some far forbidden country," the Garden of Eden from which they have been forever expelled. Our colonialists, on the verge of being deprived of their dishonestly gained and falsely cared-for Garden of Eden, now face a future of exile in a place which will no longer be a garden of pleasure for them but will become instead an alien and hostile jungle. Line twelve as it originally stood made it clear that their suffering would be caused in part by a yearning for the great capitals of the West from which they had come, but to which they would now find it difficult to retreat without losing all. Though the revised line still suggests that it is Europe for which they will suffer unrequited love, the unspecific nature of "country" allows, especially in conjunction with the indefinite "some," a fertile vagueness to develop. The forbidden home could be anywhere, perhaps even where they are, as it was in the past, before the myth was wounded and Freedom came. This vagueness is helpful because it frees us to see the universal doom of fallen man: to love that which he cannot have. In the process of revision, two definite articles are dropped, the alliteration of "cities, see" is lost, and that of "far forbidden" gained.

The transformation of "The stranger" to "A native" eliminates an ambiguity and clarifies our perspective. It is the colonialists who "walk the earth" or are "homeless, disterred"; it is they who have become strangers in the land, not those who watch them. Those who stare are strangers indeed to them but are at home in the land, native as they are not. And these natives, who in the earlier version "watch them with a happy stare," implying their own contentedness and pleased ignorance of the white man, now "disapprove them with a stare," indicating the offensiveness and impropriety of the aliens' presence.

The implied personification of the revised last line replaces the statement of the earlier version with an image. Instead of telling us that Freedom is hostile, Auden shows us this hostility in the form of a turned back, an image that to the ribald-minded may prove too graphic. One way or another, "Freedom's back in every door" can be visualized, but I find it most disconcerting to try to picture Freedom's back in every tree. Could this refer to the animals of the newly liberated garden, who no longer need fear the disarmed outsider?

XXII (*Journey to a War*)

Simple like all dream wishes, they employ
The elementary language of the heart,
And speak to muscles of the need for joy:
The dying and the lovers soon to part

Hear them and have to whistle. Always new,
They mirror every change in our position;
They are our evidence of what we do;
They speak directly to our lost condition.

Think in this year what pleased the dancers best:
When Austria died and China was forsaken,
Shanghai in flames and Teruel retaken,

France put her case before the world; 'Partout
Il y a de la joie.' America addressed
The earth: 'Do you love me as I love you'? (Auden, *Journey to a
War* 256)

XVII (*CSP*)

Simple like all dream-wishes, they employ
The elementary rhythms of the heart,
Speak to our muscles of a need for joy:
The dying and the lovers bound to part

Hear them and have to whistle. Ever new,
They mirror every change in our position,
They are our evidence of how we do,
The very echoes of our lost condition.

Think in this year what pleased the dancers best,
When Austria died, when China was forsaken,
Shanghai in flames and Teruel re-taken.

France put her case before the world: *Partout
Il y a de la joie.* America addressed
Mankind: *Do you love me as I love you*? (Auden, *CSP* 136)

Sonnet XVII (formerly XXII) has a rhyme scheme of ABAB CDCD EFF GEG, the same pattern as that found in sonnets VII and IX. All rhymes are full if we grant a somewhat anglicized pronunciation or intonation to "Partout." The poem is in regular iambic pentameter. Lines with masculine endings are decasyllabic with the exception of line thirteen, which, perhaps because it is half composed in French, is excused from the usual regimentation and displays an eleventh syllable. All four lines ending in feminine rhymes, needless to say, also display their quite legitimate eleventh syllable.

This poem seems more recalcitrantly bound to the specific events of the times than are the other sonnets preserved in this sequence. Though place names have been introduced before, notably in the chilling last line of sonnet XII, "Nanking. Dachau," they have never been as pervasive as in this sonnet, where four countries and two cities are mentioned in the last five lines. A certain symbolic and emotional force is gained from the associations of these names, but their evocative power is likely to diminish with time. The last line of sonnet XII is less likely to fade since much of its force lies in the abrupt, staccato quality of the sound, as well as in the associations of the words.

Sonnet XVII deals with the basic appeal of fascism to the instincts that dwell in all of us, "The elementary rhythms of the heart," and with the egocentric, facile optimism of the willfully blind democracies, who either proclaim, "Partout / Il y a de la joie," or coyly ask of the world, "Do you love me as I love you?" In Fuller's words, it "contrasts the essentially national self-regard of appeasement or isolationism . . . with the primitive enthusiasm of the 'dancers' . . . who appeal to 'the elementary rhythms of the heart' and 'speak to our muscles of a need for joy,' and are pleased at the events in Austria, China, and Spain: the fascist in all of us" (Fuller, *Reader's Guide* 127).

There are relatively few revisions in sonnet XVII and those that occur are minor. In the first quatrain, "The elementary language of the heart" becomes "The elementary rhythms of the heart." The change seems worthwhile for a number of reasons. "Rhythms" implies motion and emotion as the word "language" does not and is accordingly more effective in the present context. It also has a literal as well as a metaphoric meaning, whereas "language of the heart" is only a somewhat road-weary metaphor. In the next line, an initial "and" is dropped, the possessive pronoun "our" is interpolated, and "the need" becomes "a need." (Only one other conjunctive "and" and one other definite article are cut in the rest of the poem, while, most unexpectedly, a new definite article appears in revised line eight.) In the last line of the opening stanza, "lovers soon to part" becomes "lovers bound to part." The usual adverb is replaced by a verbal modifier which, while functioning as an adjective, carries with it the overtones of necessity that it has when used as a verb in its literal sense. The revision also brings into the line the linguistic irony or seeming paradox of being "bound to part."

In the first line of the second quatrain, "Always new" becomes "Ever new," ridiculing, by its proximity to "every change" in the following line, the dishonest facility and utilitarian inconstancy of the leaders and their obedient organs. In the third line there is an interesting little change from "They are our evidence of what we do" to "They are our evidence of how we do," implying that our leaders are not only our sole source of information as to whether we are winning or losing but even as to the rightness of our overall conduct. The answer to the question, "How are we doing," carries with it, to my ear, overtones of moral judgment along with the factual or technical judgement. The last line of this stanza undergoes the most extensive revision of the poem, "They speak directly to our lost condition" becoming "The very echoes of our lost condition." The revised line makes it clear that the fault lies within us, not simply in "them," for "they" exist as "echoes of our lost condition," in response to it as well as in confirmation or as a cause of it. The line now implies that "they" tell us what we want to hear: lies suggesting that we are not fallen. Our very desire for these echoes is, of course, proof of "our lost condition." The use of the image of echoes parallels or complements the mirroring in the second line of the stanza.

In the first tercet, two punctuation changes occur, the conversion of a colon at the end of the first line into a comma, and the very helpful replacement of a comma at the end of the third line with a period. In the middle line, the connective "and" is changed to "when," diminishing the sing-song quality of lines ten and eleven, with their sets of place names perfectly balanced around their matching central connectives. Now line ten has the modest rhetorical device of a repeated "when" giving a kind of incantatory intensity to it. This rhetorical repetition is not unlike that introduced to the second stanza of sonnet XVI by the four initial "Some's." It is even more reminiscent of the revision in sonnet XII, when the replacement of two "and's" in the second stanza resulted in the pounding reiteration of "Who thirst at nine who were to thirst at noon, / Who can be lost and are, who miss their wives."

In the last stanza, all quoted material, whether in French or in English, now appears in italics instead of within quotation marks. The only other change is the replacement of "The earth" in the last line by "Mankind." A definite article is eliminated and a heavy irony introduced, for now America addresses a lifeless abstraction that contains within it, quite literally and linguistically, the particular and living reality, "Mankind" enveloping and hiding the breathing "man."

XXVII (*Journey to a War*)

> Wandering lost upon the mountains of our choice,
> Again and again we sigh for an ancient South,
> For the warm nude ages of instinctive poise,
> For the taste of joy in the innocent mouth.
>
> Asleep in our huts, how we dream of a part
> In the glorious balls of the future; each intricate maze
> Has a plan, and the disciplined movements of the heart
> Can follow for ever and ever its harmless ways.

We envy streams and houses that are sure:
But we are articled to error; we
Were never nude and calm like a great door,

And never will be perfect like the fountains;
We live in freedom by necessity,
A mountain people dwelling among mountains. (Auden, *Journey to a War* 256–57)

XVII (*CSP*)

Chilled by the Present, its gloom and its noise,
On waking we sigh for an ancient South,
A warm nude age of instinctive poise,
A taste of joy in an innocent mouth.

At night in our huts we dream of a part
In the balls of the Future: each ritual maze
Has a musical plan, and a musical heart
Can faultlessly follow its faultless ways.

We envy streams and houses that are sure,
But, doubtful, articled to error, we
Were never nude and calm as a great door,

And never will be faultless like our fountains:
We live in freedom by necessity,
A mountain people dwelling among mountains. (Auden, *CSP* 136)

Sonnet XVIII was originally sonnet XVII, the final poem of "In Time of War." In the revised sequence as it appears in *CSP*, this poem has been moved forward to a position in front of the two sonnets originally numbered XXIII and XXIV, while those numbered XXV and XXVI have been dropped, the former being transplanted to the other sequence taken from *Journey to a War*, "A Voyage."

The rhyme scheme of this sonnet is ABAB CDCD EFEF GFG, the same pattern that appears in sonnets II and VIII. The only rhyme word affected by revision is "choice," which is replaced at the end of the opening line by "noise," which, with its voiced *s*, provides a full rhyme for line three's "poise." The rhymes of the two quatrains are all full masculine rhymes, but those of the tercets are linked by the consonance "sure-door," those of the second tercet by the only full feminine rhyme of the poem, "fountains-moun-tains." The middle lines of the two tercets form a light rhyme, "we-necessity," similar to one encountered in the first stanza of sonnet XII, "monument-sent," and another, "all-animal," that we will come to in the sestet of sonnet XIX.

The entire sestet of sonnet XVIII is in regular iambic pentameter; each line with a masculine ending is decasyllabic, and those with feminine end-ings adding an eleventh syllable. Revision, largely confined in this poem to the octave, in no way affects the metrics of the sestet. It does, however, have considerable effect on the metrics of the octave, each line of which is shorter in *CSP* than in the original version. In the first quatrain, the lines originally had a syllabic count of twelve, twelve, eleven, and eleven, whereas in the revised version all lines are decasyllabic save the third, which is one syllable short. All lines now consist of four feet, an unusual scansion for a sonnet sequence in which the only deviations from pentameter have been occasional Alexandrines. The first line, in fact, is reduced from an Alexandrine to a four foot line consisting of two iambs followed by two anapests. The second line is reduced from five feet to four, retaining two anapests, but losing its central iamb. The third line drops two unaccented syllables, one of which, the second syllable in "ages," had defied traditional scansion, and remains a four foot line. The last line of the opening quatrain loses one unaccented syllable at its head, trading an anapest for an iamb in the initial position, remaining, of course, a four foot line.

In the second quatrain, revision results again in four tetrameter lines. The first line, originally consisting of an iamb and three anapests, loses one syl-lable but remains a four foot line, with iambic and anapestic feet alternating. The second line sacrifices a trisyllabic adjective of dubious worth and is reduced from a five foot to a four foot line of anapests. The third line loses only one of its thirteen syllables but is reduced from five feet, consisting of three anapests and two iambs, to a four foot line of anapests. The last line of this quatrain, originally composed of three anapests sandwiched between two iambs, now is reduced to two anapests in the same iambic sandwich. The metrics of this sonnet are particularly arresting in that the predominant foot of the octave is clearly the anapest, while iambic pentameter reigns supreme in the sestet.

Originally the concluding poem in this sonnet sequence portraying fallen man's history of effort and failure, this sonnet came as the climactic point of summation, if not revelation, in which the evidence of the other poems, sifted and analyzed, was distilled, and the human condition succinctly described. It began with a marvelous image, now discarded, of mankind, of us, "Wandering lost upon the mountains of our choice," throwing us back to the first sonnet of the sequence in which man "Looked for truth but always was mistaken, / And envied his few friends, and chose his love." It continued with a description, unchanged in the revised version, of man's nostalgia for the "warm nude age" before the fall and the expulsion, and his dreams of order and joy in the future. The sestet began with lines, now slightly altered, that said, "We envy streams and houses that are sure: // But we are articled to error," reminding us again of the opening sonnet, but even more of the metaphor in sonnet II, when our progenitors, upon eating of the forbidden fruit, found "The stream was dumb with whom they'd always planned." The final stanza, only slightly changed in the revised version, went on to say that we "never will be perfect like the fountains," evoking an image from sonnet III closely related to that of the dumb stream in sonnet II: "The fountain's utterance was itself alone." The poem's conclusion, which stands untouched, proclaimed the paradox of the human condition and then, in the simple, noble language of the poetry of heroic ages, left us with this final image of ourselves: "A mountain people dwelling among mountains." The effect of all this was that, after a panoramic study of human history, with the focus upon our failures, which, as Monroe K. Spears points out, "are all, essentially, failures to achieve the truly human," (*W.H. Auden* 132), the sequence concluded with a poem which, though not overtly optimistic, did, by the very beauty of language and image in its final lines, suggest a certain nobility and worthiness in mankind. One's feeling, at the end, was like that evoked by the brave fatalistic verses of Anglo-Saxon poetry.

This poem has undergone considerable revision, particularly in the octave, but its overall tenor remains the same. However, by placing the poem in a new position, Auden has significantly altered the structure of his sonnet sequence. Formerly, this was the sequence's final, climactic poem, in which, without rosy promises for the future, the pessimism of the earlier sonnets was answered by the moving simplicity and beauty of the final human portrait. Now it appears as a kind of pivotal point, a crest from which the preceding sonnets can all be viewed, but beyond which lies more terrain that, anticlimactic as it may seem, must be traversed. Instead of being allowed to rest, having been given the human condition in succinct paradox and beautiful image, we now rather unexpectedly are confronted by the only two optimistic sonnets of the sequence. They of course gain considerable strength from their new position. In the first, Rilke, patiently awaiting the resurgence of inner light "for ten years of drought and silence," is held up as an inspiration for us in these desperate days, while in the second, the unknown, humble, natural dwellers on the earth are remembered, and their virtue offered us: "If we allow them, they can breathe again: / Happy their wish and mild to flower and flood." After these two exercises in hope, the sequence now concludes with the transposed dedicatory poem "To E.M. Forster," which, as an antidote to whatever easy optimism we may have developed, warns us again that evil dwells in all of us, whether or not we ignore the fact, and that, deny our fallen state as we may, we will be reminded of it. And, just as for our expelled progenitors in sonnet II "the way back by angels was defended," so now, "as we swear our lie, Miss Avery / Comes out into the garden with a sword." The sequence now begins and ends with gardens and forbidding swords.

The octave of sonnet XVIII is substantially revised. The beautiful mythic quality of the first line's *paysage moralisé*, "Wandering lost upon the mountains of our choice," is sacrificed in favor of a less moving but more appropriate opening line. The revised opening, "Chilled by the Present, its gloom and its noise," most effectively dampens our spirits, thrusting us immediately into the dreary, unromantic atmosphere of daily existence, while presenting a distinct, studied contrast to the "ancient South" for which we sigh in the next line. The initial participle links to the one in the next line, for it is, literally as well as figuratively, "On waking" that we are "Chilled by the Present." The mythic beauty of the original is intentionally abandoned precisely because it is into that kind of heroic, romantic atmosphere that we waft ourselves in an attempt to escape our cold factual Present. Only after demanding that we see things as they are does Auden permit himself and us the luxury and joy of the concluding stanza's magical aura of heroism and myth. In this revision, the uncompromising craftsman has exchanged a beautiful feeling of emptiness and loneliness for a less satisfying, unpleasantly contemporaneous sense of malcontent. The Grecian urn was wrong and, forced to choose, Auden picks Truth. From the purely technical side, revision of this line replaces the approximate rhyme of "choice-poise" with the full rhyme, "noise-poise."

In the second line the initial phrase, "Again and again," is replaced by the more informative and more suggestive "On waking." The sense of the original locution is maintained by the present participle, which implies the periodicity of the event. At the same time, the line now intimates that we sigh for what we apparently continue to seek while unconscious, an "ancient South," of which, perhaps, we have vague memories and intuitions in our sleep, and which, in any case, is clearly denied us by "the Present" to which we awake.

The third line is revised from "For the warm nude ages of instinctive poise" to "A warm nude age of instinctive poise." A superfluous preposition is cut, a definite article is replaced by an indefinite one, and the line's metrics are considerably simplified. Instead of an anapest followed by a spondee and a pyrrhic, with two iambs closing out the line, the verse now scans as iamb, spondee, anapest, iamb. However the gain in technical efficiency is a mixed blessing, for the looseness of the original line is probably more in the spirit of what it describes than is the tightness of the revised version. The fourth line undergoes a parallel revision, "For the taste of joy in the innocent mouth" becoming "A taste of joy in an innocent mouth." The definite articles replaced by indefinite articles are two of the six "the's" eliminated from the poem. The line, already in tetrameter in the original, retains its four feet to match the revised metrics of the other lines.

In the first line of the second quatrain, "Asleep" becomes "At night" and "how we dream" becomes simply "we dream." Probably "Asleep" came as too blatant an antithesis to the newly introduced "On waking" in line two. The unnecessary "how" is tastefully dropped. In the second line, "glorious," the modifier of "balls," is dropped. This revision allows the line to conform to the four foot standard established for the octave. More significantly, though less successfully, I believe it is an attempt to lessen the obtrusiveness of what, in a serious poem, stands out as a most inglorious pun. Auden, in revising, must have become aware of the humorous pun, but, not wanting to sacrifice the image of the great patterned dance, decided to let it stand. He probably was not too disturbed at discovering the genital joke, in any case, for in the foreword to *Bloomfield's Bibliography* he says: "Among the many varieties of badness . . . there is one which no writer can regret, the unintentionally funny line; written in all seriousness, he suddenly realizes, thanks, usually, to some friend who draws his attention to it, that the images it conjures up are of a delicious absurdity." In the same line, "future" is capitalized to match "Present" in the first line of the poem. This introduction of two capitalized abstractions into the revised version is, of course, most unusual, as Auden's tendency has been to reduce capitals to lower case whenever possible. Perhaps because this poem sums up the human condition and does so largely in terms of time, placing man squarely in the present while he yearns for past and future, Auden felt it best to give each realm its due, capitalizing all three, the past being represented by the "ancient South" of line two. The punctuation mark after "Future" is changed from a semicolon to a colon, making it clear that the description of the next two and a half lines is an elaboration of our dream (Auden, Foreword to *Bibliography* vii).

After the colon, revision is massive. The change at the end of line two is best studied in conjunction with the extensive changes in the ensuing lines:

> . . . each intricate maze
> Has a plan, and the disciplined movements of the heart
> Can follow for ever and ever its harmless ways.

After revision these lines read:

> . . . each ritual maze
> Has a musical plan, and a musical heart
> Can faultlessly follow its faultless ways.

The change from "intricate" to "ritual" implies immediately that the complexities of the dance in the future are all part of "a plan," of an order, and that the maze need not be feared as it is only part of a ritualized pattern. The yearning for order, always evident in the dream, is brought to greater prominence by this series of revisions. In line three of the stanza, the metaphor moves from the visible maze of the dance to the "musical plan" that controls it. By balancing "a musical plan" with "a musical heart," Auden implies that in this dream there is an order which we not only instinctively comprehend but to which we, in fact, belong. No longer does he speak of "disciplined movements of the heart," for "a musical heart / Can faultlessly follow its faultless ways." The human heart and the dance are so closely allied that instinct, it would seem, happily replaces discipline. This dream might well have occurred, not "at night in our huts," but among schoolchildren, for truly "How can we know the dancer from the dance?" Turning to the final line of the stanza, we find another balanced repetition to match the musical balance of the previous line. Eliminating "for ever and ever" as he had "Again and again" in line two, and converting "harmless" to "faultless," Auden puts together a four foot decasyllabic line in which three of the accented syllables alliterate, "faultlessly" and faultless" balancing gracefully on either side of "follow." The alliteration of *f*'s is accompanied by a less obvious, though more pervasive repetition of *l* sounds, six of them occurring in the single line. The technical artistry of the revision carries with it a significant shift in meaning. The paths of the maze, formerly made "harmless" by "the disciplined movements of the heart," now are "faultless," and our "musical heart" follows them "faultlessly." The introduction of the word *faultless* into the revised version firmly establishes the connection between the dream of the Future and the "sigh for the ancient South" in line two. It is now clear that what we dream will come is a lost perfection of the past, a lost paradise of order in which "musical hearts" are happy and fit for the "musical plan."

In two successive lines, Auden employs the device of repetition to create a sense of equilibrium. In both cases the reappearance of a word acts as a kind of fulfillment and answer to its first appearance, functioning as does the repetition of a melodic phrase in music. Auden has worked successfully with repetition in earlier revisions, notably in sonnets XII, XVI, and XVII, but those efforts are not, in my judgment, as ambitious and important as the ones we have just looked at. In the last line of this sonnet, Auden resorts once again to the same device and achieves a triumph.

Revision in the sestet is fairly limited. Line ten is changed from "But we are articled to error; we" to "But, doubtful, articled to error, we." Since the subject is repeated at the end of the line and a verb provided at the beginning of the next line, "we are" proves quite expendable. Its place is taken by the modifier "doubtful," the perfect antithesis of "sure," the predicate adjective of "streams and houses" in the previous line. While contrasting pointedly with "sure," "doubtful" combines nicely with "articled to error" to give an efficient thumbnail sketch of fallen man. The only other change in the stanza is the minor replacement of "like" with "as," a substitution likely motivated by a desire to avoid two identical similaic constructions, "like" appearing again in the next line.

In the last stanza only the first line is touched by revision. "Perfect" becomes "faultless," "the fountains" becomes "our fountains," and the final semicolon becomes a colon. The revised adjective obviously echoes the double use of the same word in line eight. More to the point, perhaps, it provides fine alliteration for "fountains" and, in the following line, "freedom," while contributing strongly to the repetition of *l* sounds through the two lines: "And never wi*ll* be fault*l*ess *l*ike our fountains: / We *l*ive in freedom . . . " The superlative last two lines of the poem remain unchanged: "We live in freedom by necessity, / A mountain people dwelling among mountains."

Sonnets XXIII and XXIV, the two most optimistic poems of the sequence, now follow the former concluding "mountain people" sonnet. The two sonnets which originally followed them have been eliminated, sonnet XXV, revised and under the name of "A Major Port," having been transferred to the shorter sequence taken from *Journey to a War*, "A Voyage." The transplantation of sonnet XXV and the elimination of sonnet XXVI, coupled with the relocation of the "mountain people" sonnet, conspire to give to the two poems of hope a prominence they previously lacked. Before the reorganization of the sonnet sequence, they lay rather submerged in the pessimistic aura generated by the poems around them. Not only was there the weight of twenty-two sonnets documenting the history of human failure preceding them, but following them came sonnet XXV with its undercutting opening, "Nothing is given: we must find our law," now revised to "No guidance can be found in ancient lore," followed by sonnet XXVI, an obscure study of man's lack of self-knowledge.

XXVI (*Journey to a War*)

Always far from the center of our names,
The little workshop of love: yes, but how wrong
We were about the old manors and the long
Abandoned Folly and the children's games.

Only the acquisitive expects a quaint
Unsaleable product, something to please
An artistic girl; it's the selfish who sees
In every impractical beggar a saint.

We can't believe that we ourselves designed it,
A minor item of our daring plan
That caused no trouble; we took no notice of it.

Disaster comes, and we're amazed to find it
The single project that since work began
Through all the cycle showed a steady profit. (Auden, *Journey to a War*)

Then, finally, came the climactic sonnet, but it concluded not with a promise or even a suggestion of hope in the future but, instead, with a stern, if moving, portrayal of the human present. Now, although the hopeful bent of these two sonnets is less oppressed by shadows, it still does not go unchallenged. Grimly confronting whatever optimism we may have developed, a final poem appears, the serious, though middle-keyed, admonitory "To E.M. Forster," placed anticlimactically here at the end, no doubt, to bring us back down again to the reality of our own imperfect daily lives.

XXIII (*Journey to a War*)

When all the apparatus of report
Confirms the triumph of our enemies;
Our bastion pierced, our army in retreat,
Violence successful like a new disease,

And wrong a charmer everywhere invited;
When we regret that we were ever born:
Let us remember all who seemed deserted.
To-night in China let me think of one,

Who through ten years of silence worked and waited,
Until in Muzot all his powers spoke,
And everything was given once for all:

And with the gratitude of the Completed
He went out in the winter night to stroke
That little tower like a great animal. (Auden, *Journey to a War* 257)

XIX (*CSP*)

When all our apparatus of report
Confirms the triumph of our enemies,
Our frontiers crossed, our forces in retreat,
Violence pandemic like a new disease,

And Wrong a charmer everywhere invited,
When Generosity gets nothing done,
Let us remember those who looked deserted:
To-night in China let me think of one

Who for ten years of drought and silence waited,
Until in Muzot all his being spoke,
And everything was given once for all.

Awed, grateful, tired, content to die, completed,
He went out in the winter night to stroke
That tower as one pets an animal. (Auden, *CSP* 137)

Sonnet XIX (formerly XXIII) has a rhyme scheme of ABAB CDCD EFG EFG, the same pattern as that of sonnet XIV. In the original version, the only full rhyme is that of "spoke-stroke" in lines ten and thirteen, but revision adds, in the only instance in which it extends to end words, the full rhyme of "done-one" in lines six and eight. All the other rhyme pairs utilize some form of off-rhyme. In the first quatrain, lines one and three end in the elaborate consonance of "report-retreat," in which the prefixes are identical, and two of the three remaining consonants match as well. The end words of lines two and four, "enemies" and "disease," form a light rhyme, the main stress in "enemies" falling on the unrhymed first syllable. An earlier example of this type of light rhyme in which a syllable with secondary stress is matched with a fully accented syllable is that of "monument-sent" in the first quatrain of sonnet XII. Turning to the second quatrain, we find lines five and seven ending in the modest consonance of "born-one" in the original but, as already mentioned, now end in the full rhyme, "done-one." The first lines of the two tercets end in the consonance "waited-completed," a consonance identical to that of lines five and seven. The two words in each of these rhyme pairs are no more closely linked to one another than to either of the words in the other consonance pair, so one could argue for a new rhyme scheme of ABAB CDCD CEF CEF. Though such a rhyme scheme appears reasonable enough, I have chosen to rely upon a more conventional pattern, hoping to do the intricacies of the rhyme proper justice by calling attention to the quadripartite consonance. The second lines of the tercets end in the full rhyme "spoke-stroke," while the third lines end in "all-animal," a light rhyme similar to that in stanza one.

The four lines with feminine endings all exhibit eleven syllables; those with masculine endings contain the conventional ten. Only line four is a bit troublesome, scanning as decasyllabic iambic pentameter only if one slurs the adjacent vowels in "violence," reducing the word to a convenient trochaic foot. The final line of the poem, scanning as perfect iambic pentameter in the revised version, contained an eleventh syllable in its earlier form and scanned strangely, seeming to end in a surprising, unconventional cretic.

Sonnet XIX, coming as it now does on the heels of the pivotal "mountain people" sonnet, introduces a tone of hope to the sonnet sequence as it nears its end. It begins with an extended subordinate clause, six lines long, confirming "the triumph of our enemies" in the present, but then goes on to say, in the long awaited main clause, that particularly at such a time "Let us remember those who looked deserted," for example, Rilke, "Who for ten years of drought and silence waited" until his voice returned "And everything was given once for all." The poem concludes with a moving scene in which the spent and happy poet, having successfully completed the long unfinished "Duino Elegies" in the tower of Muzot, goes out "in the winter night to stroke / That tower as one pets an animal." As Fuller says, "Rilke thus becomes a symbol of possible fulfillment even at a time of apparently total evil and violence" (Fuller, *Reader's Guide* 127). It is fitting that Auden singles out Rilke as his inspiration in a time of darkness, for it is Rilke who most influenced his poetry in the late thirties, particularly the poems of this sonnet sequence and another of the same period, "The Quest." In discussing the sonnets of *Journey to a War*, Spears gives credit to Rilke, saying: "The Rilkean sonnet becomes one of the dominant forms of the period . . . in *Journey to a War* the form is used very extensively . . . the Rilkean abrupt beginning, unfixed pronouns and imagery from mythology and legend serve to counteract what would otherwise be almost too explicit a presentation of ideas and of war reporting" (Spears, *W.H. Auden* 143).

Revision in sonnet XIX is fairly extensive. Though line one merely trades a definite article for a possessive pronoun, "all the apparatus" becoming "all our apparatus," the change is of interest as it is related to the similar revision of "all the instruments" in sonnet XV and "In Memory of W.B. Yeats." Change in line two is limited to the conversion of a terminal semicolon to a comma. Line three, however, undergoes significant revision of its nouns and its important past participal. "Our bastion pierced, our army in retreat" becomes "Our frontier crossed, our forces in retreat." The change is beneficial for a number of reasons. First of all, the line is now more accurate, if less dramatic, for in modern wars it is rare that dependence is concentrated upon a single bastion, as it might well be in medieval times. Second, the language has lost its romantic flavor and has become strictly reportorial in order to match the detached technical language of the first two lines: "the apparatus of report / Confirms... ." By replacing the dramatic "bastion pierced" with the merely factual "frontier crossed," Auden chooses to employ an intentionally sterilized, dehumanized, anti-sentimental language. The advantage is clear, for the revised line, by a triumph of imitative form, successfully conveys the cold inhumanity of war while avoiding the danger inherent in any war poem of deadening readers' sensibility through a histrionic appeal to their emotions. When dealing with horrors, art must sometimes seem to lie in order to convey the truth. Revision of this line, it should be noted, also results in the alliteration of "frontier-forces."

The change of "successful" to "pandemic" in line four effectively continues the use of clinical or technical jargon while immediately suggesting the disease introduced by the simile. As soon as we see the new adjective, we think of violence as a particularly virulent, inescapable plague to which all must succumb.

In the second quatrain, line two, though quite untouched in *Opere Poetiche*, here in *CSP* is thoroughly rewritten: "When we regret that we were ever born" becoming "When Generosity gets nothing done." Perhaps Auden felt that the original line was too trite and melodramatic and that our despair could easily be guessed without being proclaimed. Dropping our regrets, he balances the previous line's image of the successful charmer Wrong with that of futile Generosity. In this revised line we have again one of the infrequent occasions when Auden, instead of eliminating capitalized abstractions, adds one. The revision of this line, as previously remarked, changes the consonance of "born-one" to the full rhyme, "done-one." The only other change in the stanza is the conversion of "all who seemed" to "those who looked" in the third line. Since Auden has already used the word "all" once in the opening stanza and will use it two more times in the third stanza, it seems natural that he should eliminate this occurrence of the word, particularly as, in its context following the invocation "Let us remember," it comes through as rather melodramatic. The echo of the line's initial *l* is made more distinct by the new verb than it had been when carried by "all."

The first line of the third stanza, describing Rilke's patient agony, is changed from "Who through ten years of silence worked and waited" to "Who for ten years of drought and silence waited." The suffering of those years is better reflected in the revised line, where "drought," with all its overtones of emptiness, dryness, sterility, and dying, now accompanies, reinforces, and even shapes the emotion effect of "silence." The single verb "waited" more effectively conveys the long loneliness of Rilke's wait than do the almost jinglingly alliterative "worked and waited." In addition, the revised version is more accurate, since, in fact, Rilke did not accomplish much fruitful work during that dark period. The apparently minor change in preposition makes the pain of those years clearer, for while the earlier "through" implies that rain will come in the end, that the period of emptiness is only a stage along the way, the revised "for," merely factual, implies nothing and raises no hopes. The only other revision in the third stanza is the change of "all his powers spoke" to "all his being spoke" in the second line. The change makes poetry the recreation in words of the poet himself, graced by the Spirit, instead of a design created from a safe distance by a skilled worker. The end of the drought is no longer signaled by the return of an attribute but by the return of the whole articulate self, and the words that are spoken are a living part of the poet himself. This is not the first time Auden has revised away the word "power" when speaking of a creative artist. In sonnet XVI, the third line is completely changed, "an artist feels his power gone" becoming "narrators find their memory gone." Auden seems reluctant to use freely a word which, "In Time of War" particularly, carries connotations of domination and force. The present revision, however, may have been largely motivated by a desire to be faithful to Rilke's own sense of poetic inspiration. It is interesting to compare this revised line to a passage from Rilke's *Letters to a Young Poet*, in which, encouraging his young correspondent, Kappus, he says, "you will see in [your poems] your fond natural possession, a fragment and a voice of your life." In the same correspondence, Rilke counsels patience in a long passage which may well have influenced Auden in the original composition of this poem:

> *Everything* is gestation and then bringing forth. To let each impression and each germ of a feeling come to completion wholly in itself, in the dark, in the inexpressible, the unconscious, beyond the reach of one's own intelligence, and await with deep humility and patience the birth-hour of a new clarity: that alone is living the artist's life: in understanding as in creating. There is here no measuring with time, no years matter, and ten years are nothing . . . *patience* is everything. (Rilke, *Letters to a Young Poet* 20, 29–30)

Though the letter antedated considerably the ten-year drought of which Auden speaks, the image of ten years' patience is clearly set forth. It seems likely that Auden intentionally adopted Rilke's image for use in this poem in praise of him.

Since two of the last stanza's three lines are thoroughly revised, it might be simplest to present the revised stanza whole:

> And with the gratitude of the Completed
> He went out in the winter night to stroke
> That little tower like a great animal.

Becomes:

> Awed, grateful, tired, content to die, completed
> He went out in the winter night to stroke
> That tower as one pets an animal.

The first line loses two definite articles and an initial "and." In place of two abstract nouns, one of them capitalized and accompanied by a definite article, the line now is rich with five diverse and complementary modifiers that together cover the range of the poet's feelings after his voice miraculously returns to him. He is not just "grateful," but foremost "awed," convinced that God was present in his creative work. At the same time, he is "tired" and "content to die," because now both he and his work are "completed." Within the five foot compass of the original line, the revised version manages to provide us with a gamut of emotions that together fill in a portrait of the poet's inner state. Though the line is still in iambic pentameter, the series of modifiers, each separated from the next by a comma, combined with the load of six accents in the five foot line, makes it fuller, and, for all practical purposes, longer than any other line in the poem. The great length of the line and the progression of its rhythm, from the measured stateliness demanded by the first three words to the satisfying iambic beat of the second half of the line, suggest the extent of the poet's experience and convey his contentedness as, happy and spent, he awaits his rest.

Through revision, the last line of the poem drops one syllable, becoming conventionally decasyllabic. Though it now scans as perfect iambic pentameter, the original line, after a distinct caesura following "tower," concluded with a disturbing combination in "great animal" of two heavily stressed syllables followed by two weaker ones. This is replaced by a regularity and smoothness of meter that reinforce the quiet and gentle image the verse presents. Eliminated in the revision is the excessive sentimentality of "little tower" and "great animal." Our sympathies are fully aroused by the touching image of a man stroking a tower of stone and referring to it as "That little tower" evokes, with its cuteness, the beginnings of a negative reaction. Both adjectives are dropped, and the sentiment already created by the previous line's image is sustained by the introduction of the verb "pets." In his discussion of the revisions in "Sonnets from China," John Whitehead criticizes this change, declaring: "The revision of the last two lines of the Rilke sonnet (XIX) is . . . unfortunate, because, intended to be a paraphrase of a passage from a letter ('I went out in the cold moonlight and stroked little Muzot as if it were a great animal'), it is now further removed from what Rilke actually wrote." (Whitehead, "Vin Audenaire" 492). Though certainly further removed from Rilke's words, it has, I believe, in its present context become more effective. A sentimentality that may be appealing in the arch-romantic Rilke could, in a poem by the more controlled Auden, undermine its total impact. Auden's responsibility is to the truth conveyed by the spirit of his poem, and this truth may have little to do with scribal accuracy.

The thorough revision of these two lines in the final stanza seems to me an excellent example of how Auden now manages to make more efficient use of the space afforded him by his chosen form. The factors we see at work in these lines are careful word selection, replacement of constructions full of mere grammatical necessities (the first line's "and with the . . . of the . . . ") by descriptive and evocative words or phrases, and closer concern for using rhythm to reinforce emotional meaning.

XXIV (*Journey to a War*)

No, not their names. It was the others who built
Each great coercive avenue and square,
Where men can only recollect and stare,
The really lonely with the same sense of guilt

Who wanted to persist like that for ever;
The unloved had to leave material traces:
But these need nothing but our better faces,
And dwell in them, and know that we shall never

Remember who we are nor why we're needed.
Earth grew them as a bay grows fishermen
Or hills a shepherd; they grew ripe and seeded;

And the seeds clung to us; even our blood
Was able to revive them; and they grew again;
Happy their wish and mild to flower and flood. (Auden, *Journey to a War* 257–58)

XX (*CSP*)

Who needs their names? Another genus built
Those dictatorial avenues and squares,
Gigantic terraces, imposing stairs,
Men of a sorry kennel, racked by guilt,

Who wanted to persist in stone for ever:
Unloved, they had to leave material traces,
But these desired no statues but our faces,
To dwell there incognito, glad we never

Can dwell on what they suffered, loved or were.
Earth grew them as a bay grows fishermen
Or hills a shepherd. While they breathed, the air

All breathe took on a virtue; in our blood,
If we allow them, they can breathe again:
Happy their wish and mild to flower and flood. (Auden, *CSP* 137)

Sonnet XX (formerly XXIV) has a rhyme scheme of ABBA CDDC EFE GFG. Although the poem has been almost completely rewritten, and a number of end words have been changed, the rhyme scheme itself remains unaltered. A full rhyme in the first stanza is maintained, as the rhyming noun and verb, "square-stare," are replaced by the plural nouns, "squares-stairs." Whereas the first quatrain contains only perfect masculine rhymes, the second, its end words unaffected by revision, contains only perfect feminine rhymes. In the first tercet, a perfect feminine rhyme, "needed-seeded," is replaced by a consonance, "were-air." Sandwiched between is the middle line's "fishermen," making a light rhyme with "again" in the middle line of the concluding stanza. The first and third lines of that stanza end in the perfect masculine rhyme of "blood-flood." This poem presents a number of metrical revisions. In both the original and revised versions, all lines with feminine endings consist of the standard eleven syllables, though for line six to scan properly one must slur the final two syllables of "material," making them one unaccented syllable. Lines nine and eleven, having given up their feminine rhyme for a masculine consonance, have now, accordingly, become decasyllabic. In the opening quatrain, the first line had, in the original, an unexpected eleventh syllable, but the revised line is properly decasyllabic. The second line has taken on an extra syllable through revision, but a slurred reading of "dictatorial's" last two syllables preserves the line's perfect iambic pentameter. One could of course allow the line a bit of conventional irregularity and, reading "dictatorial" as five syllables, scan the line as two iambs, an anapest, and two iambs. In the last stanza, the middle line is reduced from an atypical Alexandrine to the expected iambic pentameter.

This poem begins by introducing the selfish, guilty, great men of history, whose works were always done with their own immortality in mind, the builders of "dictatorial avenues and squares" who "wanted to persist in stone forever." These men, whose names decorate the show-place plazas and boulevards of the world's dictatorships, and many of its republics as well, were "Men of sorry kennel," who "had to leave material traces" because they were "unloved." However, these men are "Another genus" from the ones we are really concerned with: selfless, nameless dwellers on the earth, men who led simple, natural lives, accepting in humility their temporary role on earth, glad to remain unknown to us, their posterity, to whom perhaps they may have bequeathed their goodness. Of them, Auden writes:

> Earth grew them as a bay grows fishermen
> Or hills a shepherd. While they breathed, the air
> All breathe took on a virtue . . .

He then concludes with a warm flow of hope culminating in the exceptional beauty of the last line: "If we allow them, they can breathe again: / Happy their wish and mild to flower and flood." In the preceding sonnet, Auden turned to the patient poet "Who for ten years of drought and silence waited," gaining hope from his courage and his ultimate triumph. Now he turns to all those nameless men of the past who have lived without defying nature, without greed or envy, in harmony with things as they are, and declares that they and their humble virtues may live in us again "If we allow them." This poem, with its concluding warm and fertile sweep, marks the point of greatest hope in the sonnet sequence, for the next and last poem is the admonitory reminder, "To E.M. Forster."

Each line of stanza one in sonnet XX is thoroughly revised, so it seems best to give both versions of the stanza immediately:

> No, not their names. It was the others who built
> Each great coercive avenue and square,
> Where men can only recollect and stare,
> The really lonely with the sense of guilt

Becomes:

> Who needs their names? Another genus built
> Those dictatorial avenues and squares,
> Gigantic terraces, imposing stairs,
> Men of a sorry kennel, racked by guilt,

In the original, the first line was unusual metrically, the other lines of its stanza all being uniformly decasyllabic. The only other line in the poem with a masculine ending that deviated from the decasyllabic norm was line thirteen, an Alexandrine. The first line's eleven syllables scanned as trochee, spondee, iamb, iamb, anapest, while the three other lines of the quatrain all scanned as regular iambic pentameter. Revision has also affected the poem's tone. The seemingly sententious rhetoric of the original is replaced by the apparently flippant disclaimer, "Who needs their names?" Of course, in both versions, the opening half line proves subtly ironic, directed as it is against those with names, not those without. However, the revised version, with its jauntily casual scorn, is particularly effective, for, when we discover who is who, around the end of the second quatrain, we must reverse our thinking and our emotions, both in direction and in tone. Apparently sneering at the lowly, the opening half line is really mocking all those who are concerned with names, preserving in a special class the selfless ones to whom names mean nothing. The second half of the line is clearly improved by revision, losing mere grammatical deadweight in exchange for the word "genus," with its suggestion of an enormous gulf between the men who forced their names upon avenues and squares, and the quiet, selfless men whose names are unknown. On the technical side, in the revised line there is one more alliterative *n* than in the original, but the alliterative effect is less noticeable, as two of the *n*'s are now hidden within words.

Revision of line two is best considered together with that of line three. Though one could perhaps argue that the revision achieves a literal logic, since avenues and squares are not by themselves truly "coercive," but can be "dictatorial," in the sense of "imperious, suited to a dictator," the point is a bit too fine. After all, emotionally speaking, avenues and squares could easily be coercive. However, when we look at the revised version of line three, with its extended description of the great public display of material power made by that other "genus," we see that the explanatory "coercive" is now superfluous and that the rather pompous "dictatorial" fits nicely with line three's modifiers, "Gigantic" and "imposing." Auden has decided, in revising, to elaborate upon the dictators' achievements, exposing in the process their pathetic need for immense, material symbols of their might. We now see, from the simple accumulation of grandiose public works, that the dictators are trying to force recognition of their name and their power. The revised third line, in which Auden piles up the evidence of their foolish vanity, replaces a line that had seemed out of place and directionless, and works to unify the stanza with its suggestive images.

In the fourth line, "The really lonely," a description eliciting great sympathy, with its implication that the dictators are the truly great sufferers, is replaced by the scornful pity of "Men of a sorry kennel," with its unavoidable doggish associations. "With the sense of guilt" is transformed to "racked by guilt." A fairly common expression, but one still enlivened by its vivid verbal, replaces a somewhat awkward locution that, in any case, applies equally well to all of us. As revision swept a definite article from line one and a connective "and" from line three, so here in line four it carries away two more definite articles.

Revision in the first two lines of the second quatrain is most conservative. In line one, the dictators' strivings for immortality through "avenues and squares" change "[they] wanted to persist like that for ever" to "[they] wanted to persist in stone for ever." This minor revision again calls attention to the ludicrous materialistic basis of thought from which the "Men of a sorry kennel" struggle to realize immortality. It contributes to the imagistic pattern of insensate things associated with the dictators, a pattern that is abruptly abandoned at the poem's midpoint, when a shift to the world of the good and natural occurs, characterized by imagery drawn from living, breathing flesh rather than inanimate stone. Line two, "The unloved had to leave material traces" becomes "Unloved, they had to leave material traces." A definite article is dropped and emphasis is placed upon the modifier by positioning it ahead of its pronoun substantive. At the same time, a confusing metrical situation best solved by stressing both syllables in the world "unloved," allowing a scansion of iamb, spondee, and three more iambs, is simply resolved into a normal iambic pentameter line.

The third line of the second quatrain is changed from "But these need nothing but our better faces" to "But these desired no statues but our faces." The alliteration of "better" with the two "but's," a kind of double consonance, is lost along with the alliteration of "need nothing." The abstraction "nothing" is replaced by the concrete image "no statues," which further elaborates the material nature of the dictators' efforts and hopes. This line marks the midpoint of the poem, both in terms of structure and content. It is the seventh of fourteen lines, and its first image is the concluding touch in a portrait of "Another genus," the truly selfish and irredeemably materialistic. While the "statues" belong to the world of those "Who wanted to persist in stone for ever," "our faces," the second image of this crucial line, belong to the world of true life, the world associated with the selfless, nameless men of the past, who persist not in stone but in spirit and flesh, through the continuity of human life. From this point on, the imagery of stone is replaced entirely by imagery of life. The two worlds that the poem deals with are distinctly segregated into the two parts of the poem, the break occurring with the second "but" of line seven: characteristic words before the break are "avenues . . . squares . . . terraces . . . stairs . . . persist in stone . . . material traces . . . statues," whereas after the midpoint come "our faces . . . dwell . . . glad . . . suffered, loved, or were. Earth . . . bay grows fishermen . . . hills . . . shepherd . . . breathed . . . air . . . virtue . . . blood . . . breathe again . . . happy . . . wish . . . to flower and flood." Even before being revised, line seven marked a turning point in the poem, but with the introduction of the word *statues* into the line, the contrast between the material and the human is concentrated and made explicit within the confines of the single line. Revision has replaced the present tense with the past, emphasizing that when the nameless ones lived, they had no desires for themselves in the future, content to know that precious life itself would continue in their posterity.

In examining the revisions in the last line of the second quatrain and the first of the following tercet, it is best to consider both lines in their full grammatical context:

> But these need nothing but our better faces,
> And dwell in them, and know that we shall never
>
> Remember who we are nor why we're needed

Becomes:

> But these desired no statues but our faces,
> To dwell there incognito, glad we never
>
> Can dwell on what they suffered, loved or were.

The last line of the second quatrain drops two unnecessary "and's" and adds the important modifier "incognito," emphasizing that these men seek no personal immortality, not even that of being remember by name. The second half of the line must be considered together with the line that follows. In the original, which I find somewhat obscure, the meaning seems to be that the nameless ones, dwelling in our "better faces," "know that we shall never / Remember" that we are their offspring and are needed to pass on the seed to the future. The less perplexing revised line clearly emphasizes the complete and willing acceptance by these good men of personal annihilation by replacing the noncommittal "know" with "glad." The list of things that they are glad we cannot dwell on, "what they suffered, loved or were," represents the spectrum of their human experience, the totality, in fact, of their lives, and makes clear the absolute nature of their surrender. The repetition of the word "dwell," already present in line eight, produces an antiphony of sound and complexity of meaning. Looked at in context, its echoed presence suggests the irreversibility of time, which permits the life-spirit of the past to dwell in the flesh (and spirit) of the present, but, by its very nature, denies those of today the possibility of dwelling in or on the lives of the past. It is the unrelenting irreversible flow of time, the central fact of life, a constant reminder of necessity, which "they," in humility, are glad to accept. It is this same incontrovertible fact which the great builders strive futilely to deny with their blocks of stone.

The next line and a half, completely untouched by revision, shows these men who accept life's limitations in complete consonance with nature, an integral part of the scheme of things: "Earth grew them as a bay grows fishermen / Or hills a shepherd."

The imagery from the middle of line eleven to the end of line thirteen is completely changed. Instead of an extended metaphor of seeds from the past reviving in the present, we now have an extended metaphor of air made virtuous by our progenitors' breathing, with the suggestion that today's blood may also be oxygenated by that virtue. The revised lines follow:

> . . . they grew ripe and seeded;
> And the seeds clung to us; even our blood
> Was able to revive them; and they grew again

Becomes:

> . . . While they breathed, the air
> All breathe took on a virtue; in our blood,
> If we allow them, they can breathe again:

The revision is affected by a helpful punctuation change, not visible above, the conversion of a semicolon in the middle of line eleven to a period, making a clean break between the preceding images and the extended metaphor. The semicolon in question was one of two in the same line, and, for that reason, a bit confusing, although logically reasonable enough, linking "Earth grew them . . . " with "they grew ripe." However, now that the extended metaphor has been changed from the vegetal to the animal world, the intervention of a full stop seems not only salutary but necessary. Among the effects of this wholesale revision in lines eleven through thirteen are the elimination of three "and's," the exchange of the full rhyme, "needed-seeded" for the consonance, "were-air," a significant rhythmic alteration in line twelve, and, in conjunction with the change in imagery, the replacement of the central word "seed" with "breathe." The first half of line twelve has an unmistakable biblical tone and rhythm in the original version, initial anapest followed by dactyl: "And the seeds clung to us." However, this monumental, mythic sound lies isolated in the midst of iambic lines, beautiful in itself, but rhythmically alien in its surroundings. In the revised version, not only is the biblical image of seed gone, but the mythic isolation of the line is exchanged for the interesting and challenging enjambment of the previous stanza's last words with the stanza's first ones. Rhythmically, the basic iambic movement of lines eleven and twelve is overlaid by a spondaic effect evoked by the meaning of the words in their present context, so that the two lines function together in the following fashion:

> Or **hills a shep**herd. **While they breathed**, the **air**
> **All breathe** took **on a virtue; in our blood**

The metrical pattern of the lines would seem to deny "they" and "all" primary stress, but the sense of the line seems to demand it for them. As a result, the iambic final foot of line eleven ties together two iambic lines, though it is itself surrounded by spondees. This metrical repetition of spondees reinforces the important logical link between the lines, the idea that "the air" which "they breathed" is the same air as "All breathe."

The repetition of the word "breathe," aided by the appropriately enjambing "air" at the end of the first tercet, welds together over the gulf of the stanza break the breaths of the special ones and those of all the rest of mankind. Auden carried over the word "seed" in the earlier version in order to link the last two stanzas, but the effect was a sluggish one, whereas in the revised version the line moves forward with a solemn joy, borrowing or imitating the tone of high fairy myth. The choice of breath as a substitute for seed is most interesting, for it indicates a desire to shift the focus from the biological aspect to the spiritual. That we are connected through the flesh with our ancestors is clear enough from the fact that they dwell in our faces incognito, so instead of using the image of the fleshly seed, Auden shifts to the image of the spiritual breath. By weaving the word *breathe* into his pattern three times in three lines, Auden achieves a quality of unity, while at the same time creating a sense of the ebb and flow movement of breathing itself.

Not only is the imagery pattern entirely revised, but the meaning is also significantly modified. It seems in the earlier version that the good ones from the past have already been revived by "even our blood" and grow again. However, in the more cautious and mature revised version, instead of a *fait accompli*, Auden holds out to us a hope when he says, "In our blood, / If we allow them, they can breathe again." So, the quiet triumphant survival of a natural and humble acceptance of life without greed and selfishness has not been definitely accomplished, as in the earlier version, but remains a possibility to be striven for by men of free will.

The last line of the sonnet remains unchanged. It is one of the most beautiful, effulgent lines in any of these poems, uniting meaning and sound in perfect harmony to convey a sense of true goodness in life: "Happy their wish and mild to flower and flood."

In revising this poem, Auden has retreated somewhat from his earlier apparent declaration of the triumph of goodness. In other sonnets of this sequence, he has retreated similarly from overly definitive pessimistic conclusions. One could generalize and say that the older Auden, having left behind the brash assuredness of youth, has abandoned his earlier doctrinaire tone of certainty, whether that certainty involves a pessimistic or optimistic attitude, and tends now to emphasize that, whether things look bad or good, the door is never closed, the contest not yet over, and man remains free in this difficult world to choose his spiritual fate.

To E.M. Forster
(*Journey to a War*)

Here, though the bombs are real and dangerous,
And Italy and King's are far away,
And we're afraid that you will speak to us,
You promise still the inner life shall pay.

As we run down the slope of Hate with gladness
You trip us up like an unnoticed stone,
And just as we are closeted with Madness
You interrupt us like the telephone.

For we are Lucy, Turton, Philip, we
Wish international evil, are excited
To join the jolly ranks of the benighted

Where Reason is denied and Love ignored:
But, as we swear our lie, Miss Avery
Comes out into the garden with a sword. (Auden, *Journey to a War* 5)

XXI (*CSP*)
(To E.M. Forster)

Though Italy and King's are far away,
And Truth a subject only bombs discuss,
Our ears unfriendly, still you speak to us,
Insisting that the inner life can pay.

As we dash down the slope of hate with gladness,
You trip us up like an unnoticed stone,
And, just when we are closeted with madness,
You interrupt us like the telephone.

Yes, we are Lucy, Turton, Philip: we
Wish international evil, are delighted
To join the jolly ranks of the benighted

Where reason is denied and love ignored,
But, as we swear our lie, Miss Avery
Comes out into the garden with a sword. (Auden, *CSP* 138)

Sonnet XXI, subtitled "To E.M. Forster," is the concluding poem of "Sonnets from China," having been transposed from its original position as the dedicatory poem of *Journey to a War*. Its rhyme scheme of ABBA CDCD EFF GEG, with differing rhyme patterns in the quatrains, is unique in the sonnet sequence, though "Hong Kong," "A Major Port," and parts of "A Voyage," sport similar unconventional combinations in their octaves. This variation from the practice standard for the sonnet sequence enters only with revision, for in the original version both quatrains follow a pattern of rhyming alternate lines. The end words of the first quatrain have been changed from "dangerous, away, us, pay" to "away, discuss, us, pay." The rhyme sounds of lines one and two have been reversed, and "dangerous," a light rhyme for "us" has been replaced by "discuss," a full rhyme. The rhymes of the second quatrain remain unchanged, the first and third lines ending in the full feminine rhyme, "gladness-madness," the second and fourth in what technically is a light rhyme but in practice functions as a full rhyme, "stone-telephone." The vowel of the final syllable in "telephone" suffers no change in quality from the fact that its syllable receives only a secondary stress, and, as a result, the two words make a perfect rhyme. In most of the other instances of light rhyme encountered in this study, the absence of a primary stress on the last syllable of one of the words actually changes the vowel sound, so that it is no longer identical with that in the accented syllable of its rhyme word. This shift in vowel sound can be seen in the rhyme pair, "animal-all," and, to a lesser degree, in "monument-sent." Another example of light rhyme appears in the tercets, "we" of line nine being paired with "Avery" of line thirteen. Lines ten and eleven end in a full feminine rhyme "delighted-benighted," the former replacing "excited," the end word of the original. Lines twelve and fourteen surround "Miss Avery" with a full masculine rhyme, "ignored-sword." Revision affects the metrics of none of the lines. Throughout the poem, iambic pentameter is maintained in a most regular fashion, masculine lines are uniformly decasyllabic, those with feminine endings exhibiting the expected eleventh syllable. Only line ten offers some irregularity, demanding either a scansion of the last two syllables of "international" as one, or presenting the reader with an unexpectedly lengthened line: "With **in**ter**na**tional **e**vil, **are** de**ligh**ted."

This poem in praise of E. M. Forster contrasts the wartime present and its madness, in which "Truth [is] a subject only bombs discuss," with the quiet sanity and uncompromising virtue of Forster's creative work. It shows us ourselves, "As we dash down the slope of hate with gladness," and declares that we, like the selfish, inflexible, unimaginative, ungiving characters in his novels, contribute to and help create "international evil" by choosing, for our convenience, a blindness "Where reason is denied and love ignored." But though "Our ears [are] unfriendly," Forster still speaks to us, "Insisting that the inner life can pay." And as we "swear our lie," rejecting goodness, unrelenting truth pursues us in the stern figure of Miss Avery, who "Comes out into the garden with a sword." Miss Avery is the wise old housekeeper in *Howard's End*, who appears in the final scene bearing the ancestral sword with which upper class Charles Wilcox has, in anger, accidentally killed aspiring outsider Leonard Bast. Confronted by her admonitory figure, we remember man's first disobedience and his expulsion from the Garden of Eden, and the fact that "the way back by angels was defended." In our beginning is our end.

The circle of the sonnet sequence is now completed. Beginning with the myth of the fall, the sequence has carried us through a history of western civilization reenacting that fall, to a series of sketches from contemporary times showing man's nature quite unchanged. After the still point of the recapitulatory "mountain people" sonnet came the two exercises in hope. And now, having dealt with mythical and historical past, international present, and the possibilities for a truly human future, the sequence concludes by bringing us back to ourselves, ordinary people in the ordinary world of today, guilty of evil in the ordinary ways. In bringing us down to the quotidian present, the final sonnet makes clear our integral connection to mythical and historical past and to international present, while holding up E. M. Forster and his silent, domesticated Fury, Miss Avery, as guides to a possible better future.

Major revision of sonnet XXI is confined largely to the opening quatrain, which is thoroughly recast. Since lines one and two, as well as being revised are entirely reversed, and since the revisions in lines three and four are of significant proportions, it would be best to look at the revised stanza as a whole:

> Here, though the bombs are real and dangerous,
> And Italy and King's are far away,
> And we're afraid that you will speak to us,
> You promise still the inner life shall pay.

Becomes:

> Though Italy and King's are far away,
> And Truth a subject only bombs discuss,
> Our ears unfriendly, still you speak to us,
> Insisting that the inner life can pay.

Only the "bombs" of the original's first line are salvaged, the rest, presumably considered superfluous, being discarded. That "bombs are real and dangerous" can be assumed, and the emphasis of "Here" is not needed as Auden's words could apply equally well to any war-torn land, even Italy itself, for with bombs dropping it would be "far away" from the romantic Italy and quiet Cambridge of Forster's novels. In place of the original first line, Auden moves forward, virtually unchanged, the original's second line. The revised second line is basically all new, preserving only "bombs" from the eliminated first line. The bombs now serve in a line whose grammatical subject "Truth" is "a subject only bombs discuss." The implication of the new line is that, though the reality of war presents might or power as the only truth, Forster speaks of another truth. The ensuing lines make clear that even over the sound of bombs he still speaks, "Insisting that the inner life can pay." From the technical side, revision eliminates one "and" but leaves two, introduces the capitalized abstraction, "Truth," and replaces "dangerous" with "discuss," as the rhyme word for "us."

Revision of the third line of this stanza affects its grammatical structure, its content, and its evocative power. The line as it originally stood, "And we're afraid that you will speak to us," formed the rather prosaic third part of the compound subordinate clause with which the poem begins. Now, with the initial "and" discarded, only the elliptical construction, "Our ears unfriendly," contributes to the long opening subordinate clause. The second half of the line is now composed of the first quatrain's long delayed main clause. In the original version, one had to wait until the fourth line for the main clause. Along with these grammatical changes, revision has introduced a synecdochal image in place of direct statement, the image, "our ears unfriendly," nicely suggesting "our" frightened unwillingness to listen. This effective image is followed by the actualization in the present tense of what, in the original, had been a fear couched in future tense. The alliterating "still" has been borrowed from the last line of the stanza, but its function remains unchanged. Now that the main clause has been moved up to the second half of line three, line four consists of a participial phrase that explains what it is Forster says to us. In accordance with the general tendency toward moderation noted throughout the revised sonnet sequence, line four now holds out a possible hope in place of an assured one. Instead of a "promise" that the inner life "shall pay," Auden now has Forster "Insisting that the inner life can pay." Forster's power, if anything, is increased by the new verbal, while at the same time his message is reshaped to fit reality, for one can always hope but, "doubtful," never be "sure." As "insisting" replaces "promise," the alliteration of "promise-pay" is lost, but that of "insisting-inner" takes its place.

Revision in the rest of this sonnet is much more limited. In the first line of the second quatrain, "run" becomes "dash," a generalized verb giving way to one with particular and appropriate connotations. "Dash," with its suggestion of childhood impetuosity, clearly establishes the tone for this stanza's first two lines, a tone supported by "gladness" and "trip us up," terms quickly associated with younger days. The sharp ironic contrast between the spirit of youthful play and that of worldwide hatred and mass war is accentuated by the revised verb. At the same time, the frightening element of passionate abandon common to wild games of youth and international paranoia and hatred is more sharply focused. This revision of a general, unevocative verb to a specific, suggestive one is a typical example of Auden's concretizing and particularizing tendency throughout his revisions. Earlier instances of such verbal revisions are found, for example, in sonnet VII, "walked" becoming "stalked" and "looked" becoming "glared." In this same line, "Hate" is reduced to lower case, gaining force by its modest retreat into the body of the verse's image. A similar conversion of capitalized abstraction to lower case human emotion or condition occurs in line seven, in the case of the word "Madness." In that same line, commas are added around the dependent clause, and "just as" becomes "just when," avoiding the momentarily misleading suggestion that the phrase is a simile. The latter change also serves to avoid a repetition of the stanza's opening word "As."

The conversion of the sestet's opening word from "For" to "Yes" reminds us that the poem is addressed to Forster. In the next line, the replacement of "excited" with "delighted" reduces a line with diabolical glimmers ("we . . . are excited / To join") to one of ironic conventionality, utilizing a light and smooth platitude: "[we] . . . are delighted / To join the jolly ranks." The elimination of capitals on "Hate" and "Madness" in the second stanza is matched by the reduction to lower case of their opposites, "Love" and "Reason," in the last stanza. The only remaining revision is the replacement of the definite article with the indefinite as modifier for Miss Avery's sword. Fuller considers the revision unfortunate: "The sword (sadly now given an indefinite article like much else in revised standard Auden) is *the* sword with which Charles Wilcox felled and accidentally killed Leonard Bast in *Howard's* (sic) *End*" (*Reader's Guide* 128). It is, however, also the sword, flaming at the gates of Paradise, which reminds us of our fallen nature. It seems to me that the image of Miss Avery silently carrying a sword "into the garden" sufficiently evokes memories of that other garden and other sword so that a definite article is quite unnecessary. In fact, since the garden retains a definite article, Auden may have felt that another one would have been a rather too forceful pointer to what should already be clear.

Conclusion

Upon meeting someone whom one has not seen for a time, one often feels that he has changed but cannot tell how. One may even remain in doubt as to whether the change is internal or external, profound or superficial. But the fact of a change is indisputable. When one encounters the revised version of a familiar poem, one's experience is similar. However, in the case of the poem, one can return to the original version and, by comparing the old and the new, discover, at least technically, exactly what has changed. Having isolated the revised elements, one can study them in an attempt to understand what new quality they contribute to the poem and how they achieve their effect. Such an investigation should lead to a greater understanding of poetry, of how it functions and lives, and, thus, to a greater enjoyment of it.

Auden considered a knowledge of the workings of poetry one of his proudest assets: "Vain? Not very, except / About his knowledge of metre / And his friends" (Auden, *City Without Walls* 30). The first question which interested him upon reading a poem, he said, "is technical: 'Here is a verbal contraption. How does it work?'" Clearly, he agreed with a quotation from Goethe which he included in *The Viking Book of Aphorisms,* and which might well have served as an epigraph for this work: "He who does not know the mechanical side of a craft, cannot judge it." Nor, might I add, can he fully appreciate it (Auden, *Dyer's Hand* 50).

Having decided to work with the extensively revised poems from *Journey to a War*, I concentrated upon a comparison of the original poems with their revised versions in *Collected Shorter Poems (CSP)*. I paid little attention to the discarded sonnets and ignored the abandoned verse commentary, a lengthy, overly explicit addendum to the sonnets of "In Time of War," for it seemed to me that omitted works would not reveal much about the process of the poet's craft and the manner in which his poems function. It was through examining actual revisions that I felt most could be learned about the mechanics of the living poetic organism.

In the course of the study I found that the poems I worked with, though clearly revised, remained always recognizably themselves. Their overall impact, however, had changed. The principal cause of this change seems to be twofold: besides the pervasive shift in tone from youthful assuredness to mature balance and clear-sightedness, which I have pointed out several times during my analysis, there is the highly significant change in context these poems have undergone.

The change in tone resulting from revision involves a sure-handed adjustment of the overconfident declarations of youth by a wiser and more moderate sensibility. The roughness and shrillness of extreme positions have been tempered by the broader considerations and understanding of the mature poet. Where the young man was sure of everything, the revising poet is sure only of what he truly knows. Auden's authority was firmer in his later life because it was self-limiting. What he could not know, he left in the realm of possibility, presenting to our hopes and doubts a realistically open-ended situation. The tone of the revised poems is one of reason and balance. No longer confronted by the personality of the poet, but believing his vision accurate, we face the reality of our human condition. In the original, the tone was one of rather arrogant self-assurance. All judgments were severe and definitive. We felt ourselves in the presence of cocky, precocious youth. More than reality, we felt the presence of the living poet in his poems. This feeling was encouraged by the accompanying diary of Christopher Isherwood which spoke most ingenuously of the companions' feelings.

These poems have undergone a profound change in context in being salvaged from the Isherwood-Auden collaboration of 1938 and being placed in Auden's selection of his shorter poems, *CSP*. In *Journey to a War* they were part of an integral work reflecting the personal experiences of two young Englishmen witnessing an important moment in history. They were part of a book that was a mixture of journalistic reportage, travel story, semi-autobiography, historical interpretation, and art. In *CSP* they are marshalled into place as part of a major twentieth-century poet's opus.

Journey to a War was written just before Isherwood and Auden left their native England for America. They were actually, as well as metaphorically, in the middle of the journey of their lives. Isherwood had never been to a war before, Auden had been a non-combatant on the periphery of the fighting in Spain. Both were excited to be on the far side of the world, writing their accounts "where the bombs are real." The youthful exuberance of their venture comes across most clearly through the immediacy of Isherwood's personal account. His prose diary of their experiences forms the bulk of *Journey to a War* and is often closely related to the poems. Auden and Isherwood both kept diaries and Isherwood referred to both in constructing the final version. A number of Isherwood's prose reflections, recorded separately in "Escales," reappear in some of Auden's poems. All in all, it is evident that the two men were very close at the time and that the book they produced was a true collaboration.

Journey to a War appeared in 1939 with an initial press run of 2,960 in London and 3,000 in New York. All of the poems Auden contributed to this book appeared again, largely unrevised, in his *Collected Poetry* (1945) and *Collected Shorter Poems* (1950). Besides appearing without the accompanying prose diary and extensive photographic commentary of *Journey to a War*, these poems underwent one other significant change. While the sonnet sequence with verse commentary, "In Time of War," remained intact, the shorter sequence, "London to Hongkong," was disbanded, its six poems scattered throughout the collection, their positions determined alphabetically by their first lines. The dedicatory poem "To E.M. Forster" was subjected to similar treatment. As a result, although "In Time of War" retained its integrity, the other poems from *Journey to a War* were presented only as individual, disconnected poems. The continuity of the travel impressions of "London to Hongkong" was lost, the gradual development of the contrast between West and East, the haves and the have-nots, was lost, and the sonnet to E. M. Forster became considerably less intelligible as a result of its isolation out of context. This denial of the original unity of the poems seems to suggest that Auden was at that time dissatisfied with the flavor of the earlier book, while still interested in preserving the poems he had contributed to it.

In *CSP* Auden reunited the "London to Hongkong" sequence and included the dedicatory sonnet to E. M. Forster as the terminal poem of the larger sonnet sequence, while dropping six sonnets and the entire verse commentary that followed the sonnet sequence. These changes strengthened the poems, which had been isolated in the 1945 and 1950 collections, by returning to them some of the associations and connections they had in their original context. The spirit of the earlier collaboration, however, seems to have been forgotten, its immediate concerns being supplanted by more general and universal considerations. Both sequences, for example, have been significantly retitled. "London to Hongkong" gives up its factual travelogue title for the more universal "A Voyage," while at the same time dropping its most personal poem, "The Traveller." "In Time of War," bereft of its verse commentary, loses the historical specificity of its original title for the less vivid, if less restricted, "Sonnets from China." In the first instance particulars of place are eliminated, in the second particulars of time. Together the changes shift our attention from an actual trip to a specific place at an historical moment in time to the more universal suggestions and implications that were always inherent in the situation and the poems, though originally overshadowed by the immediate appeal of exotic facts and current events. This shift of interest away from the actual events autobiographically recorded in *Journey to a War* is furthered by the fact that the two sequences are separated in *CSP* by ten intervening poems, including the much anthologized "Musée des Beaux

Arts." This apparently arbitrary interposition of alien poems written during the same general period leads one to the conclusion that Auden, wishing to preserve most of the poems written during the China trip, preferred to free them, as much as possible, from the limitations of their original context. By reuniting the poems from the "London to Hongkong" section, he increased their effect, as they all deal with the same developing theme. By separating this section from the larger sonnet sequence in *CSP*, he drew attention away from a particular journey to a particular war. Good and evil, evolution, nature and artifice, and the human condition remain, but little is left of a specific trip to a distant war made by two young and rather romantic poet-journalists in 1938. Though the revised poems utilize specific images more than the originals and gain in power as a result, they are no longer anchored to the historical and personal specifics of *Journey to a War*. They are now part of W. H. Auden's collected shorter poems, to be read as such. To a considerable degree, these poems as they appear in *CSP* have left *Journey to a War* behind.

My study, it should be clear, has dealt not with the fate of *Journey to a War* but with revisions of the poems preserved from that book. By comparing old and new words, cadences, phrases, and constructions, I have attempted to identify all changes in these poems and then to understand their purpose and gauge their effect. The transformation of "Under a padded quilt he closed his eyes" to "Under a padded quilt he turned to ice" reveals something about the diverse effects of different imagery. The conversion of "His generous bearing was a new invention" to "His carefree swagger was a fine invention" demonstrates how a whole new tone and atmosphere can be achieved by a shift in language and, accordingly, imagery. The replacement of "The rivers flooded or the Empire fell" by "A river flooded or a fortress fell" illustrates the evocative superiority of the limited and tangible over the vast and abstract, while presenting a fine lesson in the euphony of balanced alliteration. The concentrated growth of "And he became the shabby and demented" to "Grown seedy, paunchy, pouchy, disappointed" exemplifies the efficient use of a line, as well as demonstrating the importance of words' connotations and sound. The elimination of the single word "the" from the line "Certainly praise: let the song mount again and again" shows how a slight revision may affect the rhythmic movement of a line to add new energy, life, and meaning to the line. The apparently minor conversion of "The gardeners watched them pass and priced their shoes" to "Thin gardeners watched them pass and priced their shoes" makes clear how a single adjective can illuminate an image and give it dimensions and suggestions it previously lacked.

Discoveries like these were the aim of this work and its great joy. For someone who loves poetry, it is only natural to search among a poem's words and sounds and their relationships for the source of its living power. This study is, in my eyes, such a search.

Bibliography

Alvarez, A. "Rejection of Things Past." *The Observer Weekend Review*, 27 November 1966, p. 27.

Alvarez, A. *The Shaping Spirit*. London: Chatto & Windus, 1958.

Auden, W. H. *About the House*. New York: Random House, 1965.

————. *A Certain World*. New York: The Viking Press, 1970.

————. *City Without Walls*. New York: Random House, 1969.

————. *Collected Shorter Poems: 1927–1957*. New York: Random House, 1967.

————. *The Dyer's Hand*. London: Faber and Faber, 1963.

————. *Opere Poetiche*. Milan: Lerici Editori, 1966.

————. "Rilke in English." *New Republic*, C (Sept. 6, 1939), pp. 135–136.

————. Letter to Alexis Levitin. September 8, 1971.

————. Letter to Alexis Levitin. September 29, 1971.

————. Manuscript version (typed) of "City Without Walls." Undated.

Auden, W. H. and Isherwood, Christopher. *Journey to a War*. London: Faber and Faber, 1939.

Auden, W. H. and Kronenberger, Louis. *The Viking Book of Aphorisms*. New York: The Viking Press, 1962.

Bartlett, Phyllis. *Poems in Process*. New York: Oxford University Press, 1951.

Bayley, John. *The Romantic Survival*. London: Constable, 1957.

Beach, Joseph Warren. *The Making of the Auden Canon*. Minneapolis: University of Minnesota Press, 1957.

Blair, John G. *The Poetic Art of W.H. Auden*. Princeton: Princeton University Press, 1965.

Bloomfield, B. C. *W.H. Auden: A Bibliography*. Charlottesville: University Press of Virginia, 1964.

Bloom, Robert. "The Humanization of Auden's Early Style." *PMLA*, LXXXIII (May 1968), pp. 443–54.

Brooks, Cleanth. "W.H. Auden as a Critic." *Kenyon Review*, XXVI (Winter 1964), pp. 173–89.

Callan, Edward. "W.H. Auden: The Farming of a Verse." *Southern Review,* III (1967), pp. 341–55.

Carey, John. "Unpolitical Auden." *New Statesman,* LXXII (23 December 1967), p. 941.

Connolly, Cyril. "Laureate of Anglo-Saxony." *Sunday Times* (London), 27 November 1966, p. 24.

Davie, Donald. *Articulate Energy.* London: Routledge & Kegan Paul, 1955.

Deutsch, Babette. *Poetry Handbook.* New York: Grosset and Dunlap, 1962.

Ellman, Richard. *Eminent Domain.* New York: Oxford University Press, 1967.

Eliot, T. S. *The Use of Poetry and the Use of Criticism.* London: Faber and Faber, 1933.

Fuller, John. *A Reader's Guide to W.H. Auden.* New York: Farrar, Straus & Giroux, 1970.

Fraser, G. S. "Auden: The Composite Giant." *Shenandoah,* XV (Summer 1964), pp. 46–59.

Hamilton, G. Rostrevor. *The Tell-Tale Article.* London: Heinemann, Ltd., 1949.

Hampshire, Stuart. "Doctor Auden." *New York Review of Books,* February 15, 1968, pp. 3–4.

Hecht, Anthony. "Writers' Rights and Readers' Rights." *Hudson Review,* XXI (Spring 1968), pp. 207–11.

Hoggart, Richard. *W.H. Auden.* (Publication of the British Council) London: Longmans, Green & Co., Ltd., 1957.

Hough, Graham. "MacNeice and Auden." *Critical Quarterly,* IX (Spring 1967), pp. 9–17.

Isherwood, Christopher. *Exhumations.* New York: Simon & Schuster, 1966.

Kenner, Hugh. "Artemis and Harlequin." *National Review,* IXX (26 December 1967), pp. 1432–33.

Levy, Allan. "In the Autumn of the Age of Anxiety." *New York Times Magazine,* August 8, 1971, pp. 10–43.

Martin, Graham. "Mountains of Instead." *Listener,* LXXVII (23 February 1967), pp. 267–68.

Moore, Marianne. *A Marianne Moore Reader.* New York: The Viking Press, 1961.

Nitchie, George. *Marianne Moore.* New York and London: Columbia University Press, 1969.

Ostroff, A., ed. "A Symposium on 'A Change of Aim'" *Kenyon Review,* XXVI (Winter 1964), pp. 190–208.

Parker, Derek. "Auden and MacNeice." *Poetry Review,* LVIII (Summer 1967), pp. 157–59.

Poets at Work. (Introduction by Charles D. Abbott) New York: Harcourt, Brace & Co., 1948.

Quesenbery, William Doyle, Jr. "Variant Readings in W.H. Auden's Poetry." Unpublished Ph.D. dissertation, Columbia University, 1970.

Rodway, A. E. and Cook, F. W. "An Altered Auden." *Essays in Criticism,* VIII (July 1958), pp. 303–19.

Rosenthal, M. L. "Comment." *Poetry,* CXIV (May 1969), pp. 126–29.

Shapiro, Karl. "The Auden Forgeries and the Pound Index." *Prairie Schooner,* XXXII (Spring 1958), pp. 73–75.

Smith, Grover, Jr. "Review." *South Atlantic Quarterly,* LVII (Summer 1958), pp. 380–81.

Spears, Monroe K. *The Poetry of W.H. Auden.* London, Oxford, New York: Oxford University Press, 1968.

Spears, Monroe K., ed. *W.H. Auden: A Collection of Critical Essays.* Englewood Cliffs, N.J.: Prentice-Hall, 1964.

Unterecker, John. "In Praise of Excellence." *Massachusetts Review,* X (Winter– 1969), pp. 200–204.

Whitehead, John. "Vin Audenaire." *Essays in Criticism,* XVII (October 1967), pp. 487–95.

Whitman, Walt. *Leaves of Grass.* Edited by Malcolm Cowley. New York: The Viking Press, 1969.

———. *Complete Poetry and Selected Prose.* Edited by James E. Miller. Boston: Houghton Mifflin Company, 1959.

Wordsworth, William. *The Prelude.* Edited by Ernest de Selincourt. London: Oxford University Press, 1950.

Wright, George T. "A General View of Auden's Poetry." *Tennessee Studies in Literature,* X (1965), pp. 43–64.

Yeats, W. B. *The Letters of W.B. Yeats.* Edited by Allan Wade. New York: Macmillan Co., 1955.

———. *Variorum Edition of the Poems of W.B. Yeats.* Edited by Peter Allt and Russell K. Alspach. New York: Macmillan Co., 1957.

Index

About the House (Auden), 17, 22
adjective(s): sonnet V, 67; sonnet XIII,
    97, 99; sonnet XIX, 115–16; sonnet
    XXI, 121; sonnet XXVII, 128. *See
    also specific sonnet/poem*
adverb: sonnet XIII, 99; sonnet XXI,
    120; sonnet XXII, 125. *See also
    specific sonnet/poem*
alliteration/alliterative effect, 8;
    "Hongkong," 40; "Macao," 43; "The
    Ship," 33; sonnet VII, 80; sonnet
    XIX, 116; sonnet XVI, 103; sonnet
    XVIII, 109; sonnet XXI, 120; sonnet
    XXIII, 137–38; sonnet XXVII,
    132; "To E.M. Forster," 151; "The
    Voyage," 28
and. *See* conjunction(s)
The Anglican Theological Review, 14
"As I Walked Out One Evening"
    (Auden), 8, 10
Auden, W. H., 7–16; authority, 154;
    demagoguery, 10; Isherwood and.
    See Isherwood, Christopher; as
    "poet's poet," 8; self-deprecating
    poetry, 10; sonnet sequence, 11;
    verse, 10, 15. *See also specific
    sonnet/poem*

banks and poor houses, 46–47

Bloomfield, B. C., 19, 20, 38, 131

"The Cave of Making" (Auden), 22
A Certain World (Auden), 17, 21
change. *See specific poem and sonnet*
"A Change of Air" (symposium on
    Auden), 17
China, 1–2
Christianity, 15
Clemson University, 11
Collected Poems (Auden), 8, 9, 11
Collected Shorter Poems, 1927–1957
    (*CSP,* Auden), 2, 46–47, 153. *See
    also specific poem/sonnet*
colon. *See* punctuation(s)
Columbia University, 16
comma. *See* punctuation(s)
conjunction(s), 47, 146; "Macao," 43;
    sonnet I, 52, 54, 55; sonnet III, 60,
    61; sonnet IV, 63, 64; sonnet V, 68,
    70, 71; sonnet VI, 74, 76, 77; sonnet
    VII, 79, 81; sonnet VIII, 83, 84–85,
    86; sonnet XIII, 98, 99; sonnet XVI,
    104; sonnet XVII, 112; sonnet XVIII,
    109; sonnet XXI, 120, 123; sonnet
    XXIV, 146; sonnet XXVII, 131. *See
    also specific sonnet/poem*
creative writing, 15–16

About the Authors

Alexis Levitin has published forty-eight books in translation, mostly poetry from Portugal, Brazil, and Ecuador. In addition to five books by Salgado Maranhao, his work includes Clarice Lispector's *Soulstorm* and Eugenio de Andrade's *Forbidden Worlds*, both from New Directions. He is a recipient of two NEA translation fellowships and has served as a Fulbright lecturer at the Universities of Oporto and Coimbra, Portugal, The Catholic University in Guayaquil, Ecuador, and the Federal University of Santa Catarina, in Brazil. In addition, he has held translation residencies at the Banff Center, Canada, The European Translators Collegium in Straelen, Germany (twice), and the Rockefeller Foundation Study Center in Bellagio, Italy. He received his PhD in English from Columbia University in 1971. During a fifty-one year career, he taught English at Dartmouth, Tufts, Colby, Denison, and SUNY-Plattsburg, where he retired as Distinguished Professor five years ago.

Joshua Kulseth graduated with his BA in English from Clemson University and MFA in poetry from Hunter College. He received his PhD in poetry from Texas Tech University in May 2023. He is currently a lecturer at Clemson University. Joshua has given conference presentations on the poetry of Stephen Crane, Michael Longley, Robert Lowell, Sylvia Plath, and Ovid. His poems have appeared and are forthcoming in *Tar River Poetry, The Emerson Review, The Worcester Review, Rappahannock Review, The Windhover,* and others. His book manuscript, *Leaving Troy,* was shortlisted for the Cider Press Review Publication Competition. For additional information on his work, please see the attached *curriculum vitae.*